THE TEN COMMANDMENTS

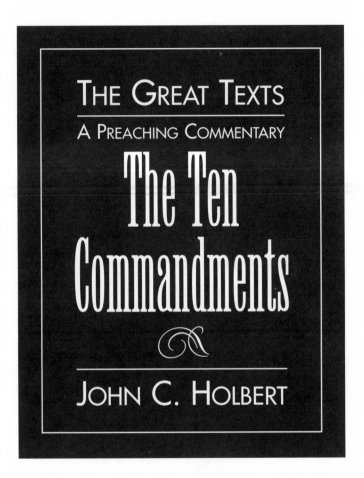

THE GREAT TEXTS

A PREACHING COMMENTARY

The Ten Commandments

JOHN C. HOLBERT

Abingdon Press

Nashville

THE GREAT TEXTS SERIES
THE TEN COMMANDMENTS
A PREACHING COMMENTARY

Copyright © 2002 by Abingdon Press

This book is printed on recycled, acid free, elemental-chlorine–free paper.

Library of Congress Cataloging-in-Publication Data

Holbert, John C.
  The Ten Commmandments : a preaching commentary / John C. Holbert.
    p. cm.
  ISBN 0-687-09048-2 (pbk. : alk. paper)
  1. Ten commandments--Homiletical use. 2. Ten commandments--Commentaries. I. Title.
  BS1285.5 .H65 2002
  222′.16077--dc21

2002003779

02 03 04 05 06 07 08 09 10 11—10 9 8 7 6 5 4 3 2 1

MANUFACTURED IN THE UNITED STATES OF AMERICA

Contents

For My Mother

Preface

A justice of the Alabama Supreme Court, Roy Moore, staunchly defends his right to display the Ten Commandments in his courtroom, suggesting that their very presence will create "a more civil atmosphere in a sometimes decidedly uncivil place." This court official has himself gone to court to defend his right to display them, believing that human law is deeply rooted in God's law, especially as that law is revealed in the Ten Commandments.

"This much is certain: anyone who knows the Ten Commandments perfectly knows the entire Scriptures. In all affairs and circumstances he (she) can counsel, help, comfort, judge, and make decisions in both spiritual and temporal matters. He (she) is qualified to sit in judgment upon all doctrines, estates, persons, laws, and everything else in the world."[1]

The Ten Commandments continue to generate the most disparate responses, from numerous jokes to adamant defense. Though it is extremely unlikely that many Christians could actually recite the Ten Commandments, and fewer still recite them in the order in which they appear in Exodus 20 and Deuteronomy 5, they remain the very hottest of religious topics at the beginning of the twenty-first century. That modern judge mentioned above is only one of many deeply religious people who are determined to make widely public this ancient list, to display them on school room doors, federal buildings, restaurants, places of business of all kinds. Such displays, these advocates say, will somehow make the world a better place. Many of the Ten are shattered so often in the modern world that supporters of public display believe just seeing them, reading them, or reciting them would somehow improve the moral fiber of the nation.

It is a commonplace to say that this great interest in, and deep controversy about, an ancient and hallowed code is a direct result of the seeming dissolution of traditional behavior in the modern world. "Honor your father and your mother?" Kids seem so disrespectful of all authority today that their parents are often treated more like impediments to the kids' desires than people worthy of honor. "You must not kill?" After the bloodiest century in the world's history—six million Jews slaughtered in World War II—twenty million Russians tortured, starved, slain in concentration camps in their own country—two million Thais killed by their own leaders—one million ethnic Hutus annihilated by Tutsis living beside them in Rwanda for years without problem—and on and on and on. It is darkly humorous to say "you must not kill" after such a record of carnage wrought by humans against their own kind. "You must not steal?" Some sort of property theft occurs every three seconds in the U.S. High profile theft of military secrets, of funds given for charity, and of the good names and reputations of many fill the pages of our newspapers every day. "You must not commit adultery?" I need cite no statistics or offer salient vignettes to demonstrate that such a command carries little genuine weight in our modern world. Perhaps it is no wonder that so many are anxious that this flood tide of moral disaster, as they see it, be dammed (or damned?). Perhaps the simple posting of the ancient Ten may be the finger in the dike needed by a society bent on its own moral demise.

Enter the preacher. These commandments are in her Bible—twice, the only list of moral laws so duplicated. Obviously, they were very significant to those who wrote them, collected them, and transmitted them in two distinct forms. She is responsible, as a transmitter of the biblical faith, to address them, to communicate them, to indicate to her people what role they may play now in our modern lives. But how? Many sermons merely shout the commandments at congregations, saying no more than, "Just say No!" Just don't kill. Just don't covet. Such sermons have contributed to the view that all religion is good for is to tell us what we ought not do; it's just a long list of "don'ts." And as we saw above, merely knowing the commandments, being aware, however dimly, of their existence, is hardly a guarantee that we will not engage in the proscribed and prescribed behavior. Despite Luther's hyperbolic claim that "to know the Ten Commandments perfectly" will lead to the right to judge "everything else in the world," the Ten Commandments by themselves are no magic force that will make us good. Paul was certain of that fact when he announced his own inability to do the good even when he perfectly well knew the good he was supposed to be doing (Rom. 7:14-20).

If the preacher is not merely to command the congregation by means of the commandments, then what is he to do? One tendency of preaching on the commandments is to extend their meaning to include so many different facets of human behaviors, that any distinctiveness in the commandments themselves is lost. For example, if the meaning of the commandment against killing is extended to ban the sale of alcohol which leads to broken homes, poor work, and bad working conditions for others,[2] then could one not extend the meaning to include the sale of automobiles (they can indeed lead to death) or kitchen knives (they are on occasion lethal)? A preacher may certainly be opposed to the sale of alcohol, but merely to quote the commandment against killing to support such a claim is playing fast and loose with the biblical text. The preacher needs to clarify and sharpen the meaning of the commandments lest they be made to serve all moral concerns. They are basic, but they are not sufficient by themselves.

But the question remains: What is a preacher to do with these ancient commands? That is what this slim volume is about. I hope to provide the exegetical and homiletical resources that a preacher may use to create a sermon or sermons on the Ten Commandments. The work is primarily exegetical. I shall spend the bulk of my time looking carefully at the actual words of the commandments. But more than word study, I will provide some suggestions for the broader context of the commandments, their wider relationships to other portions of the Hebrew Bible. In that way, a preacher may see rather more of the forest of which the trees of the Ten Commandments are a part, offering, I hope, richer biblical resources for the imagination of the preacher. Then, too, I will suggest ways in which the New Testament has used the commandments, and also take some brief looks at their influence in the emerging Christian church and in the ongoing Jewish community.

THE NUMBERING OF THE COMMANDMENTS

The Ten Commandments have throughout the centuries and in various faith traditions been numbered in several different ways.[3] The Jewish tradition has said that the first commandment is in fact the announcement: "I am the Lord your God...", while the second is "You shall have no other gods." They are alone in this numbering. Every other tradition, Lutheran, Roman Catholic, Reformed Christian, Orthodox Christian, say that the Jewish one and two are really together the first commandment. Thus, the second commandment, at least in the final two non-Jewish communities above, is the commandment against the making of images. However, in a further numbering twist, the Lutheran and Roman Catholic churches either do not list the graven image command at all or include it in their number one, making the second commandment taking God's name "in vain." For the reformed and Orthodox, the second commandment is the prohibition of images and the third is the denial of the use of the divine name "in vain."

For the purposes of this book, I will follow the numbering of the reformed tradition, the ordering best known to the majority of Protestant churches. That said, there is wisdom in the other systems, and I will refer to them as I examine the individual commandments.

There are, of course, two lists of the Ten Commandments, in Exodus 20 and Deuteronomy 5. These lists are not identical though they are obviously closely related. In my discussions I will compare and contrast the two lists and note the significance of the differences between them.

The shaping of such a work as this one should be obvious. The ten chapters will be given over to an exegetical look at each of the Ten Commandments. Each chapter will suggest various ways the information provided might be employed in preaching.

It seems especially fitting that a book on the Ten Commandments be dedicated to a parent, since the fifth commandment, "Honor your father and your mother," is one of the best known and best loved of the ten. I write these words on the day before my mother's eighty-first birthday. She remains, after more than eight decades of life, a vital and engaging person. In some weeks she still works at a paying job some fifty hours! Most important for me is that she has always been my best audience. Growing up, she always laughed at my wretched jokes, always remained interested in the peculiar twists and curves of my surprising life, always provided a survivor's mentality in the face of her own life which has not often been a smooth voyage on a calm sea. That survival strength she bequeathed to me. So, Mom, here is a book for you. I hope you have been, as the psalmist says, a "joyous mother of children" (Ps. 113:9), at least most of the time.

CHAPTER ONE

The First Commandment

I , YHWH, am your God, who brought you out of the land of Egypt, from the house of slavery; there must not be for you other gods over against my face. (Exod. 20:2-3 and Deut. 5:6-7)

THE CENTRAL IMPORTANCE OF VERSE 1

There is something very telling and crucially important in the Jewish tradition's notion that the first commandment is in fact only the first part of the sentence translated above. And at the same time that decision is, at least on the surface, a curious one. Exodus 20:2 and Deuteronomy 5:6, absolutely identical in language, are not "commands" at all. They are announcements, basic convictions about the nature of YHWH,[1] central claims about just who YHWH is for Israel. If you want to understand this God, you remember what this God has done for you, and you anticipate that this God will act in similar ways for you now and in the future. It is crucial for a full comprehension of the Ten Commandments to be clear about the power and significance of this first claim.

This first verse of the two lists of the Ten Commandments ensures that the Ten ought never to be heard as "merely" legislation for Israel or for us. When we examine the Ten Commandments, we are not looking at "law" in a simple sense. Whatever "dos" and "don'ts" the Ten announce, they are nuanced by and filtered through the proclamation of the first verse; unless and until I know

13

and affirm that YHWH is the God who brought me out of bondage, the remainder of the Ten are reduced to a sterile list of activities I may or may not choose to take seriously. But if I recognize and celebrate the God who is for me, who acts in my behalf, that God's demands become a central part of God's call on my life. In other words, the demands of "law," as always in the Bible, necessarily follow the gift of God, and I must keep gift and demand together if I am to take the Ten with appropriate seriousness.

It is for this reason that Genesis 1 *is* Genesis 1. The Bible's story begins not with demands nor with proof but with pure announcement, straightforward proclamation. "In beginning, God created sky and earth." The text does not stop here for discussion. No invitation is offered for someone to suggest a different view of things; there is no opportunity for a counterproposal. The reality of God's creative activity is merely announced and presumably sung by those who would enter into a community of those who would sing the same tune. Andrew Greeley says: "The fundamental insight of Israel is that God is *involved*. He is committed; he *cares* for his people...he cares passionately for them."[2] For Greeley such a view of God represents a "fundamental shift in world view" both individually and collectively.[3]

Those of us who participate regularly in Christian worship can well appreciate this basic claim. Each Sunday, usually after the offering of our gifts to God, we sing some setting of the ancient doxology: "Praise God from whom all blessings flow; praise God all creatures here below; praise God above, ye heavenly hosts; praise Father, Son, and Holy Ghost." In this song we join our community in announcing a worldview, one that flies in the face of several competing views, well known and embraced by many. If all blessings flow from God, then they do not flow from IBM or Coca-Cola or Viagra or Republicans or Democrats or pastors or husbands or wives. In the same way that the doxologies of our worship services and the first chapter of the book of Genesis function to ground all that follows in the gifts of God, so the first verse of the Ten Commandments focuses all subsequent demands through God's gifted lens.

It is, thus, not only the New Testament that teaches us about God's gift of grace. At the very start of what has long been known as the ultimate legislation of Israel, the traditionists who preserved the ancient code for us were careful to preface that code with the basic portrait of a God who loves and acts on their and our behalf. Any sermon on the Ten Commandments should announce loudly and clearly that the God who commands is *first* the God who loves and who acts for us. Deuteronomy makes this fact especially certain in a famous verse that follows the list of the Ten.

If Judaism has a credal confession, surely it is found at Deuteronomy 6:4: "Hear, O Israel: YHWH is our God, YHWH alone. You shall love YHWH with all your heart (i.e., your will and intelligence), and with all your life (i.e., your basic life force, all that you most centrally are), and with all your strength (i.e., your physical power)." This command to love God is said to be (6:1) *"the* commandment," a summary of all the commandments just enumerated. In response to the loving gift of freedom, bestowed by YHWH in the escape from Egypt (Deut. 5:6), Israel is to love God with heart, life, and strength. The Ten Commandments, along with all subsequent legislation, are merely commentary on this basic commandment to respond to God with the love God has shown first.

EXEGESIS OF THE FIRST COMMANDMENT

Though the translation of the first commandment seems simple enough, there are several places that deserve some commentary.

1

The first three words of the opening command could be translated in at least two ways. My reading, "I, YHWH, am your God" attempts to capture the slightly unusual word order of the Hebrew. The pronoun "I" occurs first in the sentence (the verb nearly always precedes the noun in Hebrew word order), and because that is so the emphasis of the sentence falls squarely on the identity of YHWH as Israel's God. The implication of the word order is that no other god can possibly be Israel's God, an implication that is made plain in the second part of the command. The more traditional reading of the words: "I am [YHWH], your God," (NRSV) while accurate, does not place a powerful enough emphasis on the central fact that YHWH and no other is the God who has acted in Egypt for Israel.

2

The second person pronouns of the commandment are all singular. This is so even though the literary contexts of both lists are plainly corporate ones. In Exodus God is ostensibly speaking to Moses, but in the verse that precedes God's speaking of the commandments, Moses has gone down the mountain, at God's request, to speak to the people (Exod. 19:25). And at the end of the list, the people are described as terrified and trembling in the face of the thunder and lightning, the blast of a trumpet, and the smoking mountain. They urge Moses to speak to them, but refuse to listen to God speaking, fearing death if they do (Exod. 20:18-21). Thus, the Exodus scene is one where Moses hears the Ten Commandments from God but is to convey them to the fearful ears of the people. The "you" of Exodus, though grammatically singular, is plainly plural in purpose, intended for the whole people.

And so it is in Deuteronomy. Moses himself speaks the list of Ten directly to the assembled people (Deut. 5:1-21), but he too uses the singular second person, even though he is speaking to the whole community of Israel. But, of course, in the unique style of Deuteronomy, Moses is speaking to far more people than those supposedly gathered at Jordan on the verge of the land of promise. "Not with our ancestors did YHWH make this covenant, but with us, we, those here today, all of us today" (Deut. 5:3). I translate very literally to make the point of the text. The author of Deuteronomy intends to make the commandments about to be given as contemporary as possible; they may have been given to the people through Moses long before the age of Deuteronomy's community, but they were given to that community just as surely as they were to the community of Moses. Thus, even though the singular is used, the intended plural includes all in every age who hear the commands and confirm their willingness to live in a community formed by them.

The author of Deuteronomy teaches the modern preacher a valuable lesson: this ancient legislation is to be appropriated as something more than a history lesson. All, in every place and time, who hear and affirm the God who loves the people and wills freedom for them from every bond of slavery, can become part of the everlasting covenant of that God, a covenant that forms a community

of love and justice. It is that God who spoke and who speaks the
Ten Commandments.

3
"Who brought you out of the land of Egypt, out of the house of slavery."

The use of this verb "go out/bring out" *(yatsa)* in connection
with the events of Egyptian bondage and freedom that stand at
the center of Israel's life and faith is broad and deep in the
Hebrew Bible. In over 130 instances, this formula in various forms
occurs. It is found in thirty of the thirty-nine books of the older
testament. Perhaps most impressively, ninety-one times we are
told that "YHWH brought Israel out of Egypt." It is impossible to
overestimate the significance of this affirmation for Israel's ongoing tradition.

It is thus crucial and fully appropriate that the formula should
appear at the head of both lists of Israel's most memorable legislation. As noted above, no sermon on the Ten can be preached without careful attention to the theological significance of this formula
as a proclamation of the nature of the God who commands.

4
"There must not be for you other gods."

Once again, several translations are possible for this phrase. One
could read: "You must not possess other gods," since the Hebrew
presents one of the ways that possession is expressed. An intrigu-
ing possibility is the translation, "You must not become other
gods," possible because the Hebrew also presents one of the ways
to express "becoming." I will return to this latter possibility in
some comments below. The most straightforward implication,
however, seems to be that if one affirms the YHWH who brought
Israel (and us) out of Egypt, one would be no less than a fool to
turn to other gods.

Yet turn to other gods Israel did, and with a regularity that is
both mind-boggling and disheartening. There is little evidence at
any time in the historical life of Israel that they maintained a single-minded and pure worship of this sovereign God. The names of
other gods changed from Baal to El to Astarte to Tammuz to the

Queen of Heaven, but another god by any other name is nonetheless not YHWH. This one who in the first commandment commands absolute loyalty received nothing of the kind from the chosen people.

Two points should be noted about this lack of loyalty. First, the command to possess no other gods implies that there are other gods to be chosen. The people of Israel did not burst from the shackles of Egypt into a pure monotheism—far from it. Their movement toward the belief in the one God, YHWH, was a long and arduous one. Every other culture of the Middle East worshiped a dizzying array of gods, goddesses, and godlets, and we would expect Israel to do likewise, at least early in their lives in the land of promise. The stories of Genesis refer to various tribal deities—the Fear of Isaac, the Shield of Jacob, for example—that surely were localized divinities. Sacred pillars and poles and other objects of stone and wood are mentioned in every section of the Hebrew Bible, from Gideon's snaring ephod (Judg. 8:27) to Laban's teraphim (Gen. 31:30-35) to Ezekiel's horror at the worship of Tammuz, a foreign fertility deity, in the heart of the great Temple of Jerusalem itself (Ezek. 8). The command to avoid other gods had genuine significance in every age of Israel's life.

The second point to be made is that the issue of idolatry is never a simple one. It is not merely a question of foolishly worshiping a block of wood as opposed to the living God. Second Isaiah has great good fun skewering such idiocies (e.g., Isa. 44:9-20). But merely choosing something or someone other than the great God of Exodus to revere is not the real problem. The more important problem is found in the *results* of such worship. What sort of person does the worship of other gods create? How does the activity of a person reveal just who or what that person worships? These questions lead us back to the first commandment. Right worship of the God who brought us out of the land of Egypt will lead us to listen to and affirm the nine commandments that are to follow. And living by those commandments will be the surest way to know whether YHWH is the one being worshiped. Again we see the union of gift and demand; God's activity for us leads to our response to the demands that God makes on us.

I noted above that a possible translation of this clause is: "You must not become other gods." This translation is reminiscent of the famous promise of the snake in the garden of Eden. He said to the woman that with her eating of the tree of knowledge she (and her man—the snake's verb is plural) will "become like gods" (or "like God"—the word is *elohim* as it is in the Ten Commandments). If the preposition that precedes the word *elohim* is read asseveratively, one might translate, "You will certainly become God!" With this reading, the phrase in Exodus and Deuteronomy would become, "You must not become another god over against me!"

The force of the story in the garden (Gen. 3) revolves around the desire and the willingness of the first couple to eat of the fruit in order to become either *like* God or precisely to *become* God. The hilarious result of their supposed ascent to divinity is their sewing of fig leaf aprons to cover their nakedness. Every Israelite hearing that, along with every person who lives in the warmer climates of the southern parts of the United States, would immediately burst out laughing. *They* know what fig leaves feel like. Perhaps No. 2 grade sandpaper might be a good analogy! One can only imagine how briefly the naked pair might be able actually to wear fig leaves next to the more tender places of their nakedness. Becoming God is in this wonderful tale far less than it is cracked up to be.

Whichever way one chooses to hear the phrase—to possess other gods or to become another god—the warning is clear. YHWH will brook no rival in the universe, because YHWH is the God, and no other, who brought Israel out of Egypt. And thus YHWH is the God who brings you and me out of our slavery, out of the houses of our bondage. No other god, and least of all those of us who think we can be our own gods, have the ability to so act for ourselves or for others.

5
"Over against my face."

My translation of the last two Hebrew words is rather awkward, because the words themselves are a bit awkward. The preposition, here translated "over against" *(al* in Hebrew), most often expresses motion or rest on or above something. Phrases like *"over* the earth" (Gen. 1:20) and *"beside* the wall" (1 Kings 6:5) are common examples. By extension, the preposition can be read adversatively: "to fight *against*" (Deut. 20:10) is an example. Thus, the first commandment says that to revere other gods is literally "to fly in the face of" YHWH, to go "against" the One who brought us out of Egypt.

Perhaps the most telling parallel use is found in Genesis 48:7. There Jacob describes the death of his beloved Rachel by saying "Rachel died *to my sorrow*" (literally "against me"). Jacob says that Rachel's death diminished him and brought to him pain and sadness. This use adds an important dimension to the preposition's appearance in the first commandment. YHWH's emotion when other gods are chosen is not only a demanding anger; there is also a sense of diminishment, a frustrating sorrow and loss. Like Jacob, YHWH is less without the chosen ones whom YHWH brought out of bondage.

The euphemism "my face" *(panai)*, meaning "me," adds to the very personal tone of the command. Of course, the Hebrews do in other places use the noun "face" as a picturesque way of expressing the first-person pronoun (see the Pss. 42:11 and 43:5 for examples). "The face of YHWH" is also a very common way to speak of the near presence of YHWH, and, as is well known, "to see YHWH's face" is an experience never to be had by any human. Even the great Moses is denied that vision (Exod. 33:23). The face of God may be seen in others, however, as Jacob's meeting with his brother Esau makes clear, if not to Jacob then certainly to us (Gen. 33:10). In short, when the commandment warns against choosing other gods over against YHWH's face, included in the warning is the long history of Israel's unique and special relationship to the divine face and all that the face entails. To choose other gods is to reject YHWH, most especially YHWH's face, the "face" that the ancient prayer of the book of Numbers so pleadingly called for (Num. 6:24-26).

One more arresting insight may be gained from the ancient translations of these last two words of the commandment. The Septuagint, the third to second century B.C.E. Greek translation of the Hebrew text, along with several other early translations, read the words: "only me" *(plen emou* in Greek). The emphasis of this near-paraphrase is YHWH's zealous uniqueness: "You must not take for yourselves strange gods, only me" reads the Septuagint of Exodus 20:3. This reading ties the first commandment rather more directly to the second commandment's prohibition against images, the chief rationale for which is YHWH's zealotry against anything or anybody who dared to challenge the unchallengeable God.

SERMONIC NOTES ON THE FIRST COMMANDMENT

The first commandment creates a rich and complex theological world. It could be said that it presents nothing less than a summary of the Bible's most basic claims about God.

1

The God of Israel is known best by the divine actions surrounding the Exodus from Egyptian slavery to freedom. The opening phrase answers the question, "Who is YHWH" by pointing to the exodus experience of Israel. Note what is *not* said. YHWH is not defined first and primarily as the creator of the skies and the earth, though that depiction will play a role in one formulation of a later commandment. YHWH is not defined first as a dispenser and guarantor of wisdom, though such a depiction is common in other parts of the tradition (see Job, Ecclesiastes for example). YHWH is not first defined as protector of the holiness and purity of Israel, as will be done in the vast reaches of the priestly traditions.

Because YHWH is first announced as the one "who brought you out of the land of Egypt," the Ten Commandments begin with the unmerited gift of God. But there is more. That unmerited gift is seen as a manifestation of God's justice and compassion for the weak and oppressed. The very first claim of the Ten is that YHWH is a freer of slaves. With that opening proclamation a reader may expect to discover an earthshaking series of claims, nothing less than a new worldview, in the words about to follow. Whenever one decides that these commandments were first spoken or written (and there is enormous debate about these issues),[4] they were always kept alive in a world where slavery was a common and fully accepted fact of life. But to begin by saying that this God is in the business of freeing slaves is to say that there may be other ways of ordering society than the accepted ones we know.

Thus, a sermon on the first commandment might emphasize the quite remarkable worldview manifested in these few words. This is a God of justice who may be found upsetting the world's hierarchies, leading slaves to freedom from those who think their power is infinite and eternal. This is a God who has proven possession of the real power, a power not to be challenged by any other god or by any human claiming to be a god.

2

A sermon could be formed around the question of the identity of "other gods." One should be careful here not to trivialize such an identity. It may, of course, be said that practically anything or anybody could become a "god" for someone: food, money, sex, drink, romantic love, TV, violence, gambling and on and on. Paul Tillich's famous claim, that one's "ultimate concern" is in reality one's god, might be a helpful check against trivialization. A daily desire for double cheeseburgers may not constitute a god, by Tillich's definition—a dietary problem perhaps, but not a god. On the other hand, drinking alcohol morning, noon, and night, becoming so drunk as to endanger one's own life and the lives of others, and destroying relationships with friends and family, would qualify as a god, a rival for the God of the first commandment. Any rival god who blinds a would-be believer to the gifts of YHWH of freedom from slavery and freedom for justice cannot be tolerated according to the first commandment. Surely, programs like Alcoholics Anonymous get this exactly right when they bid their adherents to admit first that they are powerless against (in this case) alcohol, and they must turn their lives over to a higher power. For followers of the Ten that higher power is YHWH, who brings us out of our slavery and into a life of freedom and hope.

CHAPTER TWO

The Second Commandment

You must not make for yourself an idol, no likeness of anything in the sky above, nor on the earth beneath, nor in the waters below the earth—you must not prostrate yourselves to them, nor serve them, because I, YHWH your God, am a zealous God, visiting the iniquity of parents on children to the third, even the fourth, generations of those hating me, but demonstrating steadfast love for thousands of those loving me and keeping my commandments. (Exod. 20:4-6 and Deut. 5:8-10)

The import of the second commandment seems plain enough: physical representations of any created thing, sprung from the hand of God, are strictly prohibited. The danger of such human creation is made obvious in the first clause. Representations of God's creations—fowl, beast, or fish—will inevitably become idols *(pesel)*. And when that happens, the first commandment will be shattered, God will be replaced by some other thing, and the foundational uniqueness of Israel's Egyptian experience will disappear.

This prohibition of imagery is not difficult to explain in a Middle Eastern world alive with physical representations. Some of the most brilliant objects of antiquity are exactly representations of animals, from the wonders of the tombs of the pharaohs to the graves of the Sumerians, Babylonians, and Assyrians. If this attack on imagery is very old, not far removed from the memories of Egypt, it is little wonder that an evolving religion, centered around the defeat of and escape from the great Egypt, would be most intent on separating itself from Egyptian practices. Egyptian temple walls and written scrolls were replete with images of bulls and crocodiles and birds and fish. This commandment warns against such wonders, because going down that artistic road can only lead to idolatry, a repetition of the Egyptian worship of Apis, the bull, Horus, the falcon, Anubis, the jackal. The safest way is simply to avoid such things altogether.

And yet the form in which the second commandment now appears to us suggests with certainty that Israel did not avoid image-making or the worship of images. The clear prohibition of all imagery is followed immediately by the warning that one must not prostrate oneself to such images nor serve them as masters. Why add such warnings to the absolute prohibition of making images at all unless images were in fact being made, worshiped, and served? Indeed, the remarkable story of Exodus 32 is nothing less than a narrative commentary on the second commandment. Whatever its historical provenance, whether as old as the Sinai experience, or a polemic against the northern king, Jereboam I, hundreds of years later than Sinai, the story's effect now in the canon of Scripture is to comment upon and illustrate the dangers announced in the second commandment.

As soon as Moses leaves the presence of the Israelites at the base of the sacred mountain in order to go up to talk to YHWH, the people demand that Aaron make them a "god" *(elohim)*, one who will go before them. Though they claim that it was certainly Moses who "brought them out of the land of Egypt" (32:1)—an obvious echo of the first commandment—after the little molten bull is presented to them, they shout, "These are your *elohim* who brought you out of the land of Egypt." They never say what the first commandment makes so clear: that it is *YHWH* who brought them out of the land of Egypt (32:4). And after Aaron's weak attempts to bring them back to the worship of YHWH by building an altar somewhere near the calf, the people, after a traditional YHWH worship service and a convivial dinner on the grounds, "rose up to revel" (32:6). The word the NRSV translates as "revel" (the older RSV had the milder "play") is a word built from the root *tsachaq*, a verb from which the famous name "Isaac" comes. In the delightful story of the birth of Isaac to his aged parents, the name means "laughter," a joyous chortle in the presence of the wondrous power of God. But here in Exodus the word has the meaning found in Genesis 26:8.

There Abimelech sees Isaac, whom he has been told is Rebekah's brother, "fondling" *(metsachaq)* Rebekah, who is of course his wife. Such "fondling" is only to occur between those intimately joined; there is a clear sexual nuance to the word. And the idolatrous Israelites now engage in such behaviors at the base of the holy mountain.

God is rightly enraged and directly accuses the people of engaging in calf-building, the worship of the calf, and the service of the calf in wanton sexual behaviors. In short, YHWH accuses Israel of breaking the second commandment, and by extension shattering the first, as well. The calf of Horeb has been set up in the face of YHWH, who is the real liberator from Egypt, not some bull-come-lately. Later in the story YHWH will reveal the essence of the divine self to Moses, using many of the words found in the second commandment (Exod. 34:6-7), about which we will say more below.

THE SUBSEQUENT HISTORY OF THE SECOND COMMANDMENT

My decision to follow the Reformed tradition and make idol prohibition the second commandment repeats an interesting and troubling history. The reformers of the sixteenth century (especially the radical followers of Calvin) perhaps were concerned to use the second commandment as part of their violent polemic against what they thought were the idolatries of Roman Catholicism. Certainly part of the divisions of the Reformers from their Roman Catholic brothers and sisters revolved around what came to be known as the "cult of Mary." Statues of Mary, as well as those of many saints, were repugnant to many reformers, and the second commandment became a weapon against their use. Lest we think such attacks are from times long ago, a 1923 commentary on the Ten from a respected English biblical scholar offers a lengthy assault on this so-called "cult of Mary," using the second commandment as the main ammunition.[1]

A recent book on the Ten expresses another danger of dividing this second commandment from the first. The authors say that the Reformers in their zeal made God not only completely horrified by any images that could become idols but at the same time made God so distant from human life that God could not be seen as one deeply engaged with us, as the first commandment tries so hard to express. The result is Deism, that belief in a God who probably exists somewhere, and who may have created things, but who now has withdrawn to a well-deserved retirement and will never be heard from again.[2] Surely, the very last thing in the minds of the framers and preservers of the Ten was to present a God like that!

Perhaps more important than these historical facts is the notion central to the rejection of images enshrined in the second commandment: iconoclasm. In the history of Judaism, the refusal to create images became at the same time a refusal to allow anyone else to force their images on them. This stubbornness became the essence of Jewish survival. The making of the golden calf was followed by any number of idol creations, as we noted above. Though the prophets, especially Isaiah, Hosea, Jeremiah, and Ezekiel, fulminated against idols of whatever stripe, idol creation and worship remained lively in Israel. Only with Ezra does the Bible go silent on the question of idols, suggesting that after one thousand years of struggle, the belief in the one God had finally triumphed. So when the Greek polytheists try to place an image (the infamous "abomination of desolation" of Daniel 9:27—second century B.C.E.) in the Temple of Jerusalem, the Maccabean revolt drives them away. And later when the Roman polytheists attempt to place emperor statues and eagle military standards in the Temple of Jerusalem, the result is another Jewish revolt (68–74 C.E.). The power, and danger, of iconoclasm may be traced to this second commandment.

The rejection of physical images in Judaism's subsequent history is a complex story. Certain Jewish believers were completely opposed to such images and passed that abhorrence on to those newest Middle Eastern monotheists, the Muslims. In the traditions of Islam, the rejection of physical representations is nearly absolute, which leads to Muslim artisan's brilliant abilities to make wonderously beautiful the very words and letters of the Arabic language. The Hagia Sophia mosque in Istanbul and the Dome of the Rock in Jerusalem are two notable examples of these superb gifts.

But there are, of course, superb Jewish artists (Marc Chagall and Ben Shann come to mind). A modern novel by the Jewish writer Chaim Potok, *My Name is Asher Lev*, addresses this ancient prohibition in a memorable story of an orthodox Jew who feels compelled to paint living objects, and the pain and struggle he goes through to do so.[3]

EXEGESIS OF THE SECOND COMMANDMENT

Several phrases and words of the second commandment need further comment.

1

The two words "idol" and "likeness" both have significant histories in the Hebrew Bible. "Idol" *(pesel)* is most prominent in three places. In Deuteronomy 4, Moses preaches a harsh sermon against idol-making (especially v. 15-31). Moses grounds his prohibition against idols in the fact that Israel "saw no form *(temunah)* when YHWH spoke to you at Horeb" (4:15). Because YHWH appeared without physical form to them they must not base their worship on any physical form. If Israel does stoop to idol-making, Moses warns that they will "completely perish," they will be "utterly destroyed" by the furious YHWH (v. 26). Still this grim exhortation ends with hope, because YHWH is always a "compassionate God" who, after Israel's inevitable idolatry, will "neither abandon nor destroy" them, never forgetting "the covenant with your ancestors" (v. 31).

The second prominent place for the use of "idol" is Second Isaiah, that prophet of the Babylonian exile. This unknown figure was especially keen to excoriate the idiocies of the worship of objects, so-called "gods" made with human hands. The "idols" are attacked as having no ability to do the thing that YHWH does routinely: save Israel by bringing them out of Egyptian bondage (43:16f) and finally leading them back to the land of Israel and out of their exile. Especially at 44:9-20 Isaiah mocks anyone who would "fall down before a block of wood." And at 48:5 Isaiah, in the voice of YHWH, reminds the exiles that YHWH had long ago announced what was to be; indeed, all that YHWH has planned has come to pass. YHWH did all that precisely so Israel would not say, "My idol did them; my carved image, my cast image commanded them." Hardly, says the amused YHWH, amazed that the chosen ones can be so stupid!

The third place where a significant use of "idol" is found is the peculiar story of Micah's idol in Judges 17–18. That this story is in fact an attack on foolish and dangerous idolatry is made plain at several points. First, of the eleven hundred silver pieces stolen from

Micah's mother, and returned to her by him, only two hundred are used to make the idol, though all of it was "consecrated to YHWH" (17:3). The idol is not seen to be worthy of more consecrated silver. The idol is a moveable "god," first for Micah's family and later for the tribe of Dan that steals it and the priest who serves it. The tribe maintains the idol "until the time that the land went into captivity" and "as long as the house of God was at Shiloh" (18:31). These final two notes of the story imply that Micah's idol was both a Danite deity figurine throughout the history of Israel (i.e., until the exile in the sixth century B.C.E.) as well as a deity over against "the house of God" at the sacred shrine of Shiloh.

This biblical evidence proves that "idol" *(pesel)* is a word suggesting a terrible danger to Israel, a danger that can lead to the breaking of covenant, the denial of YHWH, and the utter destruction of the people of God. The absolute prohibition against idolmaking at the beginning of the second commandment is a warning against an action that Israel apparently performed all too often throughout its checkered history with its God.

2

The first description of an idol in the second commandment is a "likeness" *(temunah)*. The basic meaning appears to be a perfect replica of an original or, in certain cases, the very form of the original itself. Again in Deuteronomy 4, the word is used each time the word "idol" occurs at verses 16, 23, and 25; Israel is warned not to make an "idol in the *form* of...." As noted above, Moses states clearly that when YHWH spoke from the holy fire, the people heard a sound, "but saw no form" (4:12). In three other places in the Hebrew Bible God is said to possess a quite recognizable "likeness." The psalmist concludes a plea for deliverance by claiming that upon awakening, "I shall be satisfied, beholding your likeness" (Ps. 17:15 NRSV). At Numbers 12:8 YHWH scolds the defiant Aaron and Miriam by announcing the uniqueness of Moses: "With him I speak face to face, directly, not with riddles; he sees the likeness of YHWH." Contrast that claim with YHWH's statement at Exodus 33:20 that "no one shall see me and live"! Eliphaz, the so-called friend of the suffering Job, orates a divine vision, part of which is a "likeness" before his eyes (Job 4:16). Knowing the would-be visionary theologian,

Eliphaz, he probably means to connect his divine visitation with that of Moses, claiming that he has in fact seen God.

Every use of the word "likeness/form" in the Hebrew Bible connects it either with the dangers of representations of physical objects, and the resulting inevitable idolatry, or to the very person of YHWH, whose likeness is seen only by the great Moses, and only at the express bidding of YHWH. The use of the two words "idol" and "likeness" together at the beginning of the second commandment yields the following formula: Likeness = idol = idolatry = destruction. The warning could not be clearer: avoid the making of idols; they lead only to your doom!

3

The warnings against "likenesses" include the traditional three-storied universe of ancient Hebrew cosmogony: "the sky above, on the earth, or under the earth." This universe mirrors the first chapter of Genesis where God creates "sky and earth," water being found both above the sky (falling as rain) and below the earth (arising as dew on the ground). These three "stories" are the loci of God's creatures from birds to beasts to fish to sea monsters. None of these may serve as models for human representation.

4

"You must not prostrate yourselves to them nor serve them." As noted above, after the complete prohibition of idol-making, the commandment goes right on to warn the people never to prostrate themselves to idols nor to serve idols, just as if the idols had actually been made!

The word I have translated "prostrate yourselves" is a very physically active verb, meaning rather more than the usual reading "worship." The appropriate posture in the ancient Near East in the presence of a superior person or being is on one's face in the dirt. It is easy to see how such a custom arose; a defeated enemy or an inferior person is completely defenseless and helpless in such a position. The hands can be seen outspread, the feet stretched out behind, presenting no chance for attack, no opportunity for sudden assault. To prostrate oneself is to announce that the person in whose presence one is is vastly superior and worthy of complete deference. When Joseph's brothers bring the young

Benjamin with them to Egypt to satisfy the demands of the terrible vizier (who is their brother Joseph in disguise), they "prostrate themselves" before him (Gen. 43:28), knowing he holds the power of life and death over them. When the Jew, Mordecai, refuses to "prostrate himself" before the mighty Haman, the latter is so enraged as to demand that Mordecai be killed for the insult (Esth. 3:2, 5). Little wonder that in ordination services of Roman Catholic and Episcopal priests, the candidates are asked to lie prostrate before the altar as a sign of their willingness to offer themselves fully in service to God.

By adding the word "serve" after the word "prostrate," the commandment attempts to emphasize that the real issue of idolatry is not merely the act of "prostrating oneself" before some would-be god, but the desire actually to serve that god, to profess that that god is one's master. Making a god for oneself leads both to prostration before it and finally to service of it. Thus, the second commandment makes the same basic warning against idolatry that the first commandment makes: the recognition of other gods leads to disaster, away from the One who brought you out of Egypt, out of slavery.

And with that latter phrase, the second commandment presents a delicious irony. YHWH in the first commandment was shown to be most centrally the "God who brings us out of Egypt." But the house of Egypt is more specifically "the house of slavery." The word translated "slavery" in the first commandment is the noun from the verb used now in the second commandment, here translated "serve." To serve an idol or other gods is once again to become a slave. YHWH did not free us from captivity in order that we fall again into slavery, into bondage to a false god. Jeremiah plays upon this theme at 2:14-17. He asks, "Is Israel a slave, some homeborn servant?" The answer is plainly no, but the fact that the land is falling into ruin at the hands of foreign enemies seems to suggest that Israel has fallen back into slavery—this time a slavery brought on by "forsaking YHWH." Also, the apostle Paul, especially in letters to the Galatians and Romans, says again and again that "for freedom Christ has set us free...do not submit again to the yoke of slavery" (Gal. 5:1). Our right service must be to the true God, the One who brings out and makes free.

5
"I, YHWH your God, am a zealous God."

This part of the second commandment has elicited an enormous amount of comment, much of it quite painful and ill-informed. The problem, of course, revolves around the meaning of a word I have translated "zealous." The more familiar translation, "jealous" is problematic. The common meaning of the word "jealous" in English is "resentfully suspicious" or "resentfully envious." Such a portrait of the God who brought Israel up from the land of Egypt is simply not indicative of the meaning of this Hebrew word. However, another English meaning of "jealous" is "watchfully guarding," as in the sentence: "She is jealous (guarding) for her rights." That meaning comes much closer to the Hebrew meaning, but because the meanings "suspicious" or "envious" are far more common, the translation "zealous" is better. "Zealous" means "eager, enthusiastic, filled with ardor or fervor."

At the same time, it cannot be denied that many uses of this adjective, and its verb and noun roots, do often contain elements of anger against YHWH's and Israel's enemies (see Isa. 42:13; 63:15; Zech. 1:14; 8:2). YHWH's zeal can be a consuming fire, a raging wrath. This fact guards readers of the second commandment from reducing YHWH's zeal to a polite "tut-tut" when Israel falls away from YHWH's command for exclusive leadership.

The essence of the word "zealous" in this context is to proclaim the deep seriousness both in YHWH's choice of Israel in the first commandment and YHWH's demand of exclusive loyalty in the second. Such seriousness is especially demonstrated by the difficult phrase that follows: "visiting the iniquity of the parents on the children to the third, even the fourth, generations of those hating me." Many have read these words and shuddered with abhorrence; how could God, creator of heaven and earth, "curse" descendants for generations for the evils done by ancient ancestors? A closer look is needed.

The claim is in reality a quite practical one: the evil that people do, people who hate YHWH and all that YHWH represents, plainly does not die with them but infects succeeding generations.

We citizens of the United States have a classic example of this truth. When Africans were brought to the British colony that later became the United States, they were packed in ships like the animals their captors thought them to be. And for over two centuries the descendants of those first slaves remained in bondage to their white owners. Their official emancipation came in the midst of the American Civil War, nearly 150 years ago. Yet, no citizen of the United States in 2002 would dare to deny that the iniquities of these long-ago white owners are with us still, in many subtle and not-so-subtle ways, economically, politically, and socially. Those owners of the seventeenth, eighteenth, and nineteenth centuries plainly "hated YHWH" in their enslavement of human beings whom the first commandment proclaims were "brought out of the house of slavery." The shattering of that commandment by the slave owners is tragically ironic. YHWH's basic announcement of freedom from slavery was flouted by the enslavement of millions of YHWH's people, and we still live with that terrible iniquity, "to the third, even the fourth, generation."

Fortunately, the command ends with resounding hope: "but doing *hesed* (steadfast love) for thousands of those loving me and keeping my commandments." Two things are worthy of comment.

The word *hesed* (the NRSV's "steadfast love") is a very important word in the Hebrew Bible. It is used some 245 times, and though many uses are secular ones, the word's use as a central definition of the character of YHWH is paramount. Zobel offers a helpful summary of the word's meaning in relation to God.

> The history of Yahweh's people, past, present, and future, the life of the individual Israelite—in fact, the entire world—is the stage for the demonstration of Yahweh's kindness. Yahweh has decided in favor of Israel; he has promised life, care, alleviation of distress, and preservation—indeed, he has filled the whole earth with his kindness. He has thus granted fellowship with him to his people, to all mankind, to the whole world. This... fellowship is characterized by permanence, constancy, and reliability.[4]

Those loving YHWH can look forward to expressions of YHWH's *hesed* "for thousands." Note the sharp difference between "third and fourth" and "thousands." YHWH's ultimate desire for the created world is *hesed*, not a flourishing iniquity. And "keeping the commandments," these very commandments, also calls forth the *hesed* of YHWH.

We must not reduce these claims to the foolish notion that all who love God and all who keep God's commandments will inevitably and always receive YHWH's favor in terms of success, victory, wealth, and happiness. The hard-eyed Hebrews would never have suggested such empty idiocies; they, like us, know the world in which they live far too well. YHWH's promise of *hesed* is YHWH's promise of connection with us, a refusal to forget about us, and a promise to keep the demands of justice and righteousness ever before us. We surely can choose "iniquity," and too often do to our deep distress, but YHWH's divine *hesed* is always available to those who take seriously the fact that they have been brought out of slavery by a YHWH who will not let them go. Only those who recognize the truth of YHWH's deliverance of them from slavery, and who join in a community of others who claim that truth, can witness the *hesed* of YHWH. The order of the commandments is crucial: first, I embrace what YHWH has done for me, and in that embrace I am empowered to see YHWH's *hesed* and to keep YHWH's commandments.

SERMONIC NOTES ON THE SECOND COMMANDMENT

There appear to be three important questions raised by the second commandment.

1

Creating and serving idols is behavior contrary to the exclusive demands of the YHWH who "brought you up out the land of Egypt." Preachers for centuries have named various objects and ideas from their own particular contexts as idols. Luther in the Large Catechism (perhaps prefiguring Paul Tillich's famous "ultimate concern") identified a god as "that to which your heart clings and entrusts itself."[5] Andrew Greeley says that idolatry comes in many guises: social causes, church authority, or "any movement, activity, commitment, interest, or concern" that can become "a substitute for God."[6] Nearly all those who comment on the second commandment agree with Luther: anything can certainly become a god for us, "if our heart clings to it."

Yet, this line of thought runs a risk of trivializing the commandment, and can lead to moralizing sermons. "Don't turn your (Golf game? Bank account? Mercedes Benz? House on the Lake? fill in the blank) into a god." Such moralizing words leave out the most important concern of the second commandment, which is the question of God. As Brevard Childs notes, the commandment raises the basic question of "what is the proper vehicle for worshiping God?"[7] Childs goes on to say the second commandment guards "the purity of God's self-revelation (in the first commandment, I assume he means) lest Israel confuse its own image with that of God's."[8] This commandment stands at the heart of the Bible's important concern to point out the myriad of threats that humans can author against the divine nature. In other words, making my bank account some sort of ultimate concern threatens to do nothing less than reject God, to deny finally that it was YHWH "who brought us out of the land of Egypt." With that denial comes practical atheism, and an inability to witness YHWH's *hesed* in my life and in the life of my community. A sermon with a title like "Who Is Your Real God?" should be certain to move beyond platitudes about "the love of money" and should focus on the profound threat to the community of love, called forth by God, that such a "love of money" can engender.

2

The whole idea of the "zeal" of God can be food for a theological sermon on God's nature. There has been so much confusion about the word "jealous," and what that could possibly mean when describing the God of Jesus Christ, that careful attention to the meaning of this word in the second commandment could prove helpful. A preacher should first "clear the decks" for the congregation concerning dangerous meanings of this word, and then should offer the profound seriousness of God's love and will for all people represented in the word's central meaning.

3

The end of the commandment needs some exploration. "The iniquity to the third and fourth generation" is a cliché for many believers, and is a stumbling block for many who have read the Old Testament. A preacher will want to address the idea about the staying power of evil from generation to generation, and will want to contrast that fact with God's desire to shower *hesed* on God's people "in their thousands."

I would suggest that each of these ideas deserves its own sermonic event; I would not try to do all of them in one sermon. In a preacher's lifetime, I hope there will be occasion to preach a series on the Ten Commandments more than once. The second commandment yields material for more than one sermon topic. Save one or more of my suggestions, along with others of your own, for the next series.

CHAPTER THREE

The Third Commandment

You must not raise up the name of YHWH your God for nothing, because
YHWH will not acquit anyone who raises up his name for nothing.

This third commandment has been so trivialized in our own time that it may prove difficult to recapture something of its profound significance. How many jokes about people playing golf on Sunday, and uttering vile language, suggesting that God's last name is really "damn," have you heard or said? To take the name of God "in vain" as the older translations had it was simply to utter swear words. Now that nearly every form of vile speech is readily available to us on our televisions at any hour of the day, does that mean we should join organizations to stop the use of foul language and thereby preserve the sanctity of the third commandment?

Andrew Greeley suggests that the third commandment speaks of the "consequences of frivolous and hypocritical religion."[1] He goes on to point to serious social consequences of the trivialization of religious speech. On the other hand, William Barclay claims that this command focuses more on individual false swearing, the need to uphold the "sacredness of every promise."[2] Barclay hardly mentions any possible social consequences beyond the concern that every individual should avoid making promises they cannot or will not keep. R. H. Charles, in similar fashion, says that the third commandment warns us "not to dishonor God by invoking his name to attest what is untrue." Such behavior, he says, "virtually amounts to atheism."[3] Edwin Poteat adds that the command points to the need for a "moral atmosphere in which man (sic) confronts God...free of flippancy, falsehood, and evasion."[4]

These four reactions to the third commandment focus in the main on the human behavior demanded, and that is fully appropriate. However, only Charles moves toward the core problem by suggesting that not to pay heed to this commandment is to slide toward atheism. To employ the name of God "for nothing" is to assume that God is in reality nothing, and possesses no power or authority in life. In effect it is to deny the first commandment. And if the first commandment is rejected, the others can have no force, since they depend on the absolute certainty that unless YHWH has brought me out of slavery, I owe YHWH nothing and have no inclination to follow the things that YHWH commands. It is little wonder that the command states that YHWH will not "acquit" anyone who raises the divine name for nothing, for those who do so imply that God is no thing in fact. This is serious business indeed! How then was the third commandment so trivialized as to make its import a question of swearing?

THE SUBSEQUENT HISTORY OF THE THIRD COMMANDMENT

The interpretation of this commandment in the church's history is well summarized by Martin Luther. "It is a misuse of God's name if we call upon the name of the Lord God in any way whatsoever to support falsehood or wrong of any kind," and he goes on to discuss the particular dangers of swearing false oaths in court. This commandment, he says, unlike the commandment against idols, "leads us outward and directs the lips and the tongue."[5] Two points should be noted about Luther's interpretation.

1

The emphasis of the commandment is on the common human behavior of lying, most especially in swearing falsely. The courtroom, that place in any society where the truth is most especially sought, is in view. Before a witness begins her testimony, she places her hand on a Bible and vows, in the sight of God, to tell the truth. If she then utters falsehood, she has in effect blasphemed the God of all truth. Other later commentators followed this line of interpretation by pointing to two passages of Scripture.

In Deuteronomy 19:15-21 a description is provided of the punishment for those who lie in a court. If a "malicious witness" (the word read "malicious" often carries the meaning "violence," a violence that calls forth the wrath of God—see, for example the story of the destruction of Sodom in Gen. 19) brings a charge against someone, and if that charge is proved, after careful consideration, to be false, "then you shall do to the false witness just as the false witness had meant to do to the other" (v. 19 NRSV). The story of Naboth's vineyard springs to mind (1 Kings 21). In the light of Deuteronomy 19, the two lying witnesses who falsely accused Naboth of blasphemy and traitorous words against the king, should themselves be taken out and stoned to death. Deuteronomy 19:20-21 tells why this harsh punishment must be carried out: "Others shall hear, and they will be afraid (an ancient example of the hope of deterrence) so that this evil thing will never again be done among you. Show no pity!" The quite desperate seriousness of this affront of false witness is demonstrated by that remarkable command, "Show no pity!" Do not allow your emotions to sway you from the necessity of rooting out those who would lie in the face of YHWH in order to destroy a fellow human being.

We should also note that the dangers of lying, always a distinct possibility, drove Israel not to trust any single witness when it comes to the adjudication of "any offense" (Deut. 19:15). "Only on the evidence of two or three (!) witnesses shall a charge be sustained" (v. 15 NRSV). Such a demand makes the burden of proof exceedingly difficult, particularly in the face of crimes that by their nature are done secretly, such as murder or adultery. Though the Hebrew Bible provides many occasions wherein capital punishment may be imposed (thirty-nine cases by one count), this demand for two or three truthful witnesses for any offense must have made the carrying out of such extreme punishment very difficult, and perhaps quite rare. Thus, that sharp demand to "show no pity" must have collided with this rigorous demand for multiple trustworthy witnesses in any court case.

2

Luther's emphasis on the "outward" concern of the third commandment, as opposed to the "inward" desire of the commandment against idolatry, demonstrates his concern to focus on the human behavior demanded by this commandment. Surprisingly, in his interpretation he focuses very little on God. That, of course, is quite natural in any discussion of a commandment to us humans; we are being asked to act in certain ways as opposed to other ways. However, there is danger in limiting our understanding of this third commandment merely to what we should do or not do. That limiting has led the church over the years to caricature the Ten Commandments as "dos and don'ts," crass legalisms from which we are made blessedly free by the coming of Jesus. Such a reading has led to no end of mischief in Jewish-Christian relations, and, more dangerously, to a misappropriation of the heart of the commandments in general and this third commandment in particular.

Brevard Childs has this right when he says, "The heart of the commandment lies in preventing the dishonoring of God. . . . God, as the source of truth, cannot be linked to falsehood and deception."[6] In fact, Childs contrasts this commandment with the later one about a "lying witness" against the neighbor by claiming that the third commandment is "radically theocentric," whereas the eighth commandment (by his counting) is more specifically about injury to another human being. By his comment Childs does not mean to imply that the latter command is only about human behavior while the former is only about God. Both commandments have both concerns. However, this third commandment has YHWH as its primary focus. Deuteronomy 6:13 makes this point well in unusual Hebrew grammar. Each part of this three-part sentence begins with the direct object, a most unusual pattern in Hebrew: "YHWH your God you shall hold in awe; him you shall serve; by his name you shall swear." Since these words directly follow the closest thing Israel ever offered toward a creed (Deut. 6:4), that command to love YHWH alone, it is appropriate to add the exclusiveness of "YHWH alone" to the demands of verse 13.

The implications of this theocentric reading are important. By swearing falsely, or by raising up YHWH's name for nothing, to trivialize it, I reject YHWH by treating God as nothing. In effect I deny that YHWH brought me out of the house of slavery, and by implication I turn to another god or to no god, which is in fact the same thing. This clear focus on YHWH as the subject of the third commandment preserves the seriousness of the commandment and prevents the easy moralization of its application.

EXEGESIS OF THE THIRD COMMANDMENT

Three central words need examination in our consideration of the third commandment.

1
"Raise up, lift up, or carry" (nasa')

This common Hebrew verb has several meanings. The physical meaning, "lifting or carrying," is perhaps the most common: for example, carrying the ark in the wilderness (Exod. 37:5) or carrying idols (Isa. 45:20). But this physical meaning very easily takes on metaphorical implications, most important for our subject at Exodus 19:4. "You have seen what I did to Egypt, and how I carried you on eagle's wings and brought you to myself." This marvelous figure contains both the physical sense of the word "carried" and the broader metaphorical sense. YHWH's carrying of Israel, lifting them out of the house of slavery in the same way that a mother eagle bears her chicks aloft to teach them to fly, becomes far more than a simple metaphor for the actions of God. It is a richly poetic figure, containing within it notions of love, support, and protection. Thus, in the same way that YHWH brought Israel out of Egypt on eagle's wings, so the third commandment demands that we who would "raise up, carry" the name of God do so only in love for that God, in support for the ways of that God, and to protect the honor of that God. When we raise up the name of YHWH, we call to the attention of those who hear One who made Israel a special people, choosing them in love to be "a realm of priests and a holy nation" (Exod. 19:6). These very commandments are the charter for that realm, the surety of that holiness. Any trivialization of YHWH's name voids the charter and calls into question both YHWH's holiness and the potential holiness of YHWH's people. In short, to raise up YHWH's name is to call forth nothing less than the power of YHWH's will for YHWH's people. Who would dare to trivialize such a name of power?

2
The "Name" of YHWH

It has been commonplace in the study of this commandment to discuss the ancient, and so-called primitive idea of the power of a name. In the garden of Eden Adam is given the power of naming all the creatures of God, thereby gaining some measure of power over them. He also names his companion "Eve," a Hebrew word having some relationship to the word for "life" or "living." The several places in Genesis where the ancestors receive new names (e.g., Gen. 17:5, 15) suggest that names have unique revelatory power, pointing to the special significance of that name's bearer. The classical place for this discussion is, of course, the revelation to Moses of the name of YHWH at the burning bush. Or, perhaps better said, the ambiguous refusal on the part of God to reveal the name at Moses' express request. "I am who I am" may be revelatory, but might just as well be a divine dodge. Whichever it is, the name of this God is eternally fascinating to the traditions of Israel, so much so that later in that tradition it is determined that to say the name at all is to do something quite dangerous.

The name is also important as a kind of living immortality. In the delightful book of Ruth, Boaz is asked by Ruth to marry her in order to keep the name of the family of Ruth's dead husband alive in the land. To destroy one's name is to extirpate one's family (Deut. 25:6; Num. 27:4). In addition, to have a name is to have a reputation, either a good one (so David at 2 Sam. 8:13) or an evil one (so Ezek. 23:10).

Though this idea is often called "primitive," and is thereby connected with magical power over another, the idea may not be only primitive. Anyone who has been called in to dinner by an irate parent, whose food is getting cold, knows well the power of a name, especially when the vowels of that named are elongated for special effect! And why is it that parents labor so long over what to name their newborn child? Because without a name, there is something important missing from that child, some distinguishing mark that makes her/him who she/he actually is. My wife and I named our firstborn Darius, much to the horror of my parents, who prayed mightily for a girl. Alas for them, Darius was a boy, and I readily admit that for the first few days of his life I wondered whether Darius was a fit name for our first child. But it soon enough became clear that he was Darius and no other. And his name now conjures up all the things he is in himself and to us. To call out "Darius" is to call on my son.

So it is with YHWH. To call out "YHWH" (or if one does not say that sacred name, some substituted word) is to call on the God who brought us out of the land of Egypt. That name is the only name by which YHWH is known. And those of us who are Christians have the same notion about the name of Jesus. Paul memorably states our conviction: "at the name of Jesus every knee should bend, in heaven and on earth and under the earth ..." (Phil. 2:10 NRSV). As the newer evangelical chorus has it: "There's something about that name!" That something for the Old Testament is the first commandment. It is that named God who brought us out of the house of slavery.

3
"Emptiness, nothingness" (shw')

This word is used in three different contexts in the Old Testament.

A General Use

In Psalm 89:46 in the midst of a caustic complaint the psalmist cries out "How long, O [YHWH]? Will you hide yourself forever? How long will your wrath burn like fire?" (NRSV). The psalmist complains that YHWH is inexplicably absent, but at the same time horribly present. YHWH's presence is demanded, but not the wrathful presence witnessed by the psalmist. Verse 47 goes on to charge, "For what emptiness *(shw')* you have created all mortals!" Life leads only to one thing, death, made all too real by the power of the fearful Sheol, the place of death (v. 48). In this psalm the word means, more precisely, meaninglessness; YHWH's wrathful presence has made the psalmist's existence appalling, worse than empty, more fearful than any imagination could create. To raise up the name of YHWH for *shw'* in this meaning is to make YHWH even worse than empty; it is to claim that YHWH is darkness and horror itself.

Emptiness of Speech

In Ezekiel 12:21-25, the prophet announces a terrifying word of YHWH. A furious YHWH confronts the prophet with a proverb YHWH has overheard. "Mortal (the literal "son of humanity"), what is this proverb ... 'The days are lengthened, and every vision comes to nothing'?" The people of Israel refuse to believe that the hard words of the prophet concerning destruction and exile are words that come from YHWH. Instead of Ezekiel's words, the people have listened to easier words about an eternal Israel, have listened to visionaries who speak soothing words of ease and comfort. "There shall no longer be any false *(shw')* vision or flattering divination within the house of Israel. But I YHWH will speak the word that I speak, and it will be fulfilled" (vv. 24-25)! A *shw'* word is by definition no word of YHWH, because YHWH has no truck with falsehood and lies. To raise up YHWH's name for *shw'* in this meaning is to connect YHWH's name with false language and lying visions, the very opposite of YHWH's desire for truth.

False Conduct

At Job 15:31 there is a delicious play on words with *shw'* at the heart of the fun. Of course, it should be noted that Job finds the word play less than fun, since it is a cruel jibe by the would-be comforter, Eliphaz, attacking the agonized sufferer on the ash heap. Though Eliphaz is engaging in what looks like a generalized "fate of the wicked" speech (vv. 17-35), much of the speech is in fact directed squarely at Job.

> Let them (the wicked) not trust in *shw'*,
> being led astray,
> because *shw'* will be their reward!

At 7:3 Job had lamented that he had been given "months of *shw'*." Eliphaz believes that Job continually condemns himself as evil with his very own words (15:6). Thus, Eliphaz hears Job complain about his *shw'*, and concludes that to believe that life is characterized by *shw'* is in fact to trust in *shw'*. Anyone who claims life is merely *shw'* is doomed to receive (what else?) *shw'*, which is an early death as Eliphaz announces in the next verse. To raise up the name of YHWH for *shw'* with this meaning is to accuse YHWH of acting only out of *shw'* and of giving only *shw'* to YHWH's people.

Thus, *shw'* is nothing, even less than nothing, and is a terrible way to abuse the name of YHWH, reducing it to a useless emptiness at best, to a beastly cruelty at worst. This word indicates again the deep seriousness of this third commandment. The NRSV's translation of this commandment "to make wrongful use of" does not begin to demonstrate the terrible results that can follow when YHWH's name is abused like this. It is no trivial thing at all to raise up YHWH's name for *shw'*!

4
"To acquit, to count as innocent" (naqah)

We can best understand the meaning of this word with reference to two narrative accounts. In the long story of Joseph in Genesis, at 44:10, the disguised vizier of Egypt (Joseph in fact) plays an unpleasant cat and mouse game with his brothers, culminating with the trick of hiding his favorite cup in the sack of his youngest brother, Benjamin. After the brothers have headed back to Canaan, Joseph sends his servant to catch up with them in order to accuse them of theft. The brothers quite rightly deny that they have stolen anything from the great man, but the servant presses his accusation. The brothers swear that if any stolen object is found in the sack of any one of them, then that thief shall die and the rest of the brothers will become slaves in Egypt. The servant of Joseph replies, "Very well! As you say, it shall be. The one with whom it is found shall be my slave; but the rest of you shall be acquitted" (using the verb *naqah*). Here is a clear legal meaning; theft is punishable by death. Those not involved in the theft are free to go.

The second narrative has David as its subject. At 1 Kings 2:9, David is on his deathbed and is charging his son and heir, Solomon, to act on behalf of his father. His very last charge to the next king of Israel is the command to murder a helpless old man, Shemei, who years ago had cursed David as he fled his traitorous son, Absalom. David spared his life then, but he has not forgotten the slight. "Therefore do not acquit him! You are a wise man; you will know what you ought to do. You must bring his gray head bloodily down to Sheol!" And with that terrible demand, the aged David dies.

Rather than a legal problem that must be remedied by legal means, this is a personal vendetta wreaked on an old enemy by a vindictive king. Nevertheless, the meaning of the word is also "acquitted," though this time guilt has nothing to do with legality. These two stories suggest the basic meaning of the word.

But at the two lists of the Ten Commandments (Exod. 20:7 and Deut. 5:11), the word has a theological context. Hence, five other passages may help our understanding. They are: Jeremiah 30:11; 46:28; Exodus 34:7; Numbers 14:18; and Nahum 1:3. In each it could be said that a pattern can be seen: "God shows mercy, but does not leave the guilty totally unpunished."[7] The five passages named are in fact only two. The two places from Jeremiah are nearly identical in formulation: YHWH will make an end of all nations, but will not destroy Israel. Nevertheless, says YHWH, "I will chastise you in just measure; I will by no means acquit you." Here the word means something like "to get off scot-free." YHWH is no soft touch, politely and sweetly forgiving all manner of behavior without consequence.

And the same portrait is drawn in the other three passages, which all derive from the same root. Exodus 34 is the classic place where YHWH is revealed as "slow to anger, filled with steadfast love," but who will "by no means acquit the guilty." Numbers and Nahum quote this same phrase with only slight variations. The tradition of YHWH's serious engagement with evil is deeply rooted in the tradition of Israel; YHWH will by no means quickly or blithely forgive and forget. By this constant reference in nearly all the ages of Israel's writing life (from Exodus to Jeremiah to Nahum), the tradition announces that YHWH is serious about sin.

And one of the very greatest of sins is to "raise up the name of YHWH for nothing." YHWH will by no means acquit anyone who has the foolish, mindless temerity to do that terrible thing.

SERMONIC NOTES ON THE THIRD COMMANDMENT

Any sermon on the third commandment will need to reckon with the obvious trivialization of its content. The idea that we ought to "clean up our language" because of this commandment needs a direct confrontation. As I have tried to indicate, the issues at stake in this commandment are far more serious and far more important to a vibrant faith.

1

A possible sermon title could be "What's in a Name?" After clearing the decks of the trivial notions mentioned above, this sermon could revolve around the significance of the name of God. Whenever we utter the name of the God we worship, what is the content of that name? I have tried to suggest that the primary content is the first commandment. God's name means God's choice of Israel out of love, demonstrated most tellingly in the action of bringing Israel out of the house of slavery. To raise this name merely for support of a political platform, for victory over one's enemies, either on the battlefield or the playing field, or for divine guidance concerning the right car to purchase, could be said to "raise up the name of YHWH for nothing."

2

Another sermon title might be: "Does God Accept Everything?" Here the central question is: does God have any standards? Are human behaviors all the same in the sight of God? How far can we go in the name of God? The issue revolves around the meaning and significance of the word "acquit," God's refusal to acquit anyone who flagrantly misuses the divine name by raising it up for nothing. Psalm 50:19-21 comes to mind in this connection. The psalmist pictures God rejecting the wicked,

> You give your mouth free rein for evil,
>   and your tongue frames deceit.
> You sit and speak against your kin;
>   you slander your own mother's child.
> These things you have done and I have been silent;
>   you thought that I was one just like yourself.
> (NRSV)

Though the psalmist does not say that God's name has been misused, the free and lying speech of the wicked is not passed over by God. They think that God is "one just like themselves," quick to lie and slander and mouth evil against family and friends. But God is far from that. The name of this God has no time for such wickedness and quickly moves to rebuke such behavior.

Of course, the most difficult thing about a sermon like this is the danger of falling into the trap of unproveability. It is not *always* the case that those who toss God's name about foolishly are in fact immediately, or even in the future, rebuked by God for their actions. Many who "raise up the name of YHWH for nothing" appear to live long and happy lives, far removed from any concern for the name or actions of God. Still, Jews and Christians believe that a flagrant trivialization of God's name makes the realization of God's realm of love and justice that much more unlikely and unattainable. Those who refuse to recognize that it is God who brought us (you and me) out of our slavery have little concern for a community that lives by those values that lead to love and justice. Not to name that God as the source of our power and our strength is to claim power and strength for oneself, leading to a dissolution of community. We need to announce regularly in our communities of worship that we affirm the important content of the third commandment. That announcement and affirmation are the glue of any worshiping community.

3

Another possibility might be: "God Is a Big Nobody." In this sermon the preacher wants to address the question: how exactly do we use God's name for nothing? Is prayer in the name of God before any political gathering such a misuse? Is prayer before a football game? Is the tag line of every recent political speech, of whatever party, "God bless America"? Does the appearance of an American flag in our sanctuary constitute a use of God's name for nothing? A chaplain's prayer before a battle? My one-time prayer before the start of a square dance?

Once the preacher has suggested ways she feels that she and the congregation may be raising up God's name for nothing, she should then suggest those ways where we can and do raise up God's name for praise and adoration and for support of the things God calls us to: actions for justice, lively and true worship, support for our weakness, challenges to our sloth, hope in our hopelessness. The third commandment should be used to challenge our cheap use of God's holy name and to warn us that the name of God should not be cast about like so much chaff. It should rather be raised as a beacon light for all who would join the community of the redeemed, all who have been brought out of Egypt.

CHAPTER FOUR

The Fourth Commandment

Remember the Sabbath day by making it holy. Six days you must serve and do all your labor, but the seventh day is Sabbath to (for) YHWH, your God. You must not do any labor, you, your son and daughter, your male and female slave, your livestock, your resident alien inside your gates. Because in six days YHWH made sky and earth, the sea and everything in them. Then He rested on the seventh day. Therefore, (or that is why) YHWH blessed the seventh day and made it holy. (Exod. 20:8-11)

Guard the Sabbath day to make it holy just as YHWH your God commanded you. Six days you must serve and do all your labor, but the seventh day is Sabbath to (for) YHWH, your God. You must not do any labor, you, your son and daughter, your male and female slave, your ox, your donkey, all your livestock, your resident alien inside your gates, in order that your male and female slave may rest as you do. You must remember that you were a slave in the land of Egypt, and that YHWH, your God, brought you out of there with a powerful hand and an outstretched arm. Therefore (that is why) YHWH, your God, commanded you to make the Sabbath day. (Deut. 5:12-15)

The fourth commandment needs to be seen in both its Exodus and Deuteronomy formulations, because there are significant differences between the two. In fact, very different sermonic interests may arise from them, as I will try to demonstrate. We turn first to Exodus.

The Exodus version of the fourth commandment begins with the word "remember." That word determines the special way this version is shaped. Exodus bids us to remember what YHWH has done

49

in the act of creation. We are commanded to act in certain ways, because YHWH has already acted in a certain way, most especially the fact that YHWH "rested" after the six days of labor that brought forth "sky, earth, sea, and everything in them." The implication of this version is that if we forget that YHWH has labored in creation and has rested after that labor, we will also forget that our labor, along with all those who normally labor with us, must be balanced by rest. One could say that the Exodus version commands, "Rest on a Sabbath! What is good enough for YHWH is good enough for you! Or do you think you are more powerful than YHWH, never needing the rest that YHWH clearly needs!" Do not forget YHWH's wondrous creation, but, more important, never forget YHWH's rest.

I think it is important to emphasize the very literal meaning of the word "rest" as we approach Exodus' fourth commandment. The word often means "desist from labor" or more colloquially "take a break." Perhaps the notion that God gets tired and needs a break from work is odd in the face of certain biblical statements that God "never slumbers" (Ps. 121:3), never "grows weary" (Isa. 40:28). Indeed R. H. Charles finds such an idea "far from being a lofty one."[1] Nevertheless, in the Exodus version of the commandment, the focus is squarely on YHWH's rest after work. That means that at the very heart of the creation of the world there is enshrined the necessity of rest from work, the deep need of all, slave and free alike, to cease work for a designated time. In other words, rest is as important as work. We will have much more to say about this below.

THE SUBSEQUENT HISTORY OF THE FOURTH COMMANDMENT (EXODUS)

Edwin Poteat describes a kind of popular history of the fourth commandment. Sabbath observance, he says, "passed from observing a moon phase to a holiday, and from holiday to worship, and from worship to law, and from law to casuistry, and from casuistry to flouting the whole business. ..."[2] Though there is more than a whiff of anti-Judaism in this description, accusing the later Jewish teachers of narrowing the command to "casuistry," a narrow, unyielding legalism, Poteat does suggest that the call for rest did too often turn into a series of proscriptions against all sorts of banned behaviors. Jewish teachers were hardly the only ones to move in these directions. Of course, Jesus, the Jew, spoke for many of his Jewish teachers and friends when he uttered the famous claim that "the Sabbath was made for human beings," and not the other way round (Mark 2:27). Not all Jews were fixated on the specific demands of Sabbath as the only way to fulfill the intent of the commandment, but, of course, not all non-Jews were free of the same fixation.

However much Poteat caricatures the history of the fourth commandment, the movement from "holiday" to a narrow casuistry can be demonstrated by a quick glance at what happened to the commandment's understanding and use. As the church became increasingly organized, and a recognized and accepted part of the Roman Empire, the Lord's Day (i.e., Sunday) became more and more a religious day. As early as 312 C.E., an edict of Constantine commanded that work must stop on the Lord's Day. The eighth century teacher, Alcuin, closely identified Sabbath and Lord's Day, and taught that all work on that day was a breach of the fourth commandment. Thomas Aquinas in the fourteenth century agreed.

But the reformers again divided Sabbath from the Lord's Day, suggesting that the former was in fact a Jewish idea that had been abrogated for Christians. Luther in the Large Catechism claimed that the "power and force of this commandment consist not of the resting but of the sanctifying, so that this day should have its own particular holy work."[3] Hence, for Luther, the Lord's Day did not reject all work but commanded holy work. With this claim, Luther would have found himself in close agreement with many Jewish teachers who insisted that "holy work" was indeed to be done on the one special day. The impact of this belief was to allow certain kinds of work to be done after all on the special day. That allowance often led to a sort of liberalizing casuistry wherein increasing activity on the Lord's Day was allowed.

The Westminster Confession of 1648, written during the height of Puritan power, once again connected Sabbath and Lord's Day, and thereby rejected what the Puritans saw as the liberalizing tendencies of the reformers. These new Sabbath laws led to the "most acute Sabbatarianism in English history,"[4] and it was that

Sabbatarianism that came to the English colonies which were to become the United States.

I have my own story of the very significant effect that this Puritan sabbatarianism had in the United States even late into the twentieth century. I moved to Dallas, Texas in 1968 to attend the seminary in which I now teach. I had never been to Texas before, having grown up in Arizona and attending college in Iowa. I was a single man, aged twenty-two, and had seldom had to fend for myself when it came to food. I arrived in Dallas on a hot August Sunday night, sometime after 9:00. I checked into my dormitory, and went out searching for something to eat. I could not find any restaurant that was open, at least where I was looking, but I did see a grocery store that stayed open until midnight. I went in and selected for purchase a can of soup, a can opener, a pot in which to cook the soup, a bowl from which I planned to eat the soup, a spoon with which to eat it, and a box of saltine crackers. I took my items to the checkout line, salivating moderately with hunger, and put them up on the counter. The person at the register looked at my items and said (in a thick Texas drawl), "Well, hon, I can sell you the crackers and the soup, but not the spoon, the bowl, the pot, and the opener." "Why not," I asked with some exasperation, desperation, and confusion. "Do you need different money for those; is there a special Texas currency for nonfood items?" I was trying to be cute, thinking she had some sort of momentary confusion about these items I needed to get my meager meal going. "It's Sunday," she said matter of factly. "Can't buy that stuff on Sunday."

Thus, I had my first confrontation with the infamous blue laws, those ancient sabbatarian demands that forbid nonfood purchases on the Sabbath or the Lord's Day, a direct fallout from the Puritan's reading of the fourth commandment in the seventeenth century. I lived in the north of England for a year (1993–94), and it was only while we were living there that the country's largest grocery chain began to open on Sundays. And this in one of the world's most overtly secular societies, where fewer than 3 percent of the population consider themselves members of churches! All such blue laws have since been repealed in America, and the English now have access to all manner of stores on Sunday, but the whiff of the power of Puritan sabbatarianism still lingers every time that a neighbor wrinkles her brow as I mow my lawn on a Sunday afternoon.

EXEGESIS OF THE FOURTH COMMANDMENT (EXODUS)

For a clearer understanding of the fourth commandment, several words need closer attention.

1
"Remember" (zakar)

This word is a very significant theological one in the Hebrew Bible. It occurs in two general contexts. Human beings are said to remember something some one hundred times, and of those one hundred, fully sixty-nine find the object of remembering to be God, or God's saving acts for the people of Israel.[5] The fourth commandment urges us to remember the Sabbath, but it is a Sabbath ordained by the actions of YHWH. Hence, to remember Sabbath is to remember YHWH who made it holy by the actions of creation and rest.

The second context is when God remembers. In most cases when this idea is expressed, God remembers a person or events that are very important for persons. In the great majority of these instances, God remembers, and words or actions of God's grace and favor follow. Perhaps the finest example of this reality is found in Jeremiah 31:20: "Is my dear son Ephraim? Is he my darling child? As often as my words are against him, I clearly remember him still. That is why I yearn for him. I must have deep compassion for him." God's unfailing memory of the chosen ones leads directly, says Jeremiah, to God's inevitable compassion (a word based on the Hebrew word "womb"). And though there are several times when God remembers in order to punish iniquity (Hos. 7:2; 9:9; Jer. 14:10; Ps. 137:7), God's memory usually leads to God's grace.

Thus, the call to remember the Sabbath day is a call to remember and act. The word is rarely limited to an intellectual concern only. Remembering leads to acting, and so it is in the fourth commandment.

2
"To sanctify, to make holy" (qadosh)

This very common word consistently means "to consecrate, to dedicate, to treat as sacred." Perhaps its more basic meaning is "apartness" or "separateness." The antonym is usually "profane" in the sense of common or ordinary. If something is "holy" or is claimed to be "holy," it is unique and is to be treated with special care and deference.

The word is used hundreds of times in the Hebrew Bible, referring to God's activities (Exod. 15:11, Ps. 68:18), God's word (Amos 4:2; Ps. 89:36), places where God dwells (Deut. 26:15; Jer. 25:30), the tabernacle and temple (Exod. 40:9; Ezek. 42:14), among many others. For YHWH to "make the Sabbath day holy" is to single this day out as uniquely special, a day not like other days. We are commanded to "remember to make the Sabbath day holy" (v. 8) in response to YHWH who has already "blessed the Sabbath day and made it holy" (v. 11); the commandment is shaped like an envelope as we respond precisely in the way God has acted. And the appropriate way to remember what God has done is to rest as God has rested.

3
"Resident alien" (ger)

The opposite of a "resident alien" is a native-born person. A *ger* is a sojourner, a newcomer, one who comes to a foreign country to live for a time or perhaps to take up permanent residence. What the Hebrew Bible makes clear over and over about this class of people is that their rights and responsibilities are ultimately little different than those for natives (see Exod. 23:12; 12:19, 48, 49; Lev. 16:29 among many others). When it comes to the celebration of Passover, a circumcised foreigner is no different than a native-born Israelite; when it comes to rest on the Sabbath there is no distinction to be made. Once again the movement toward equality and justice is pronounced in the formulation of the fourth commandment.

4
"To rest" (Shabbat)

The primary meaning of the word is "cease, desist." YHWH's gift to the world of a future after the ravages of the flood are capped with the assurance that "as long as the earth endures," the seasons and their attendant climate changes "will not stop" (Gen. 8:22). The writer of Joshua says that the very day the Israelites were able to eat "the produce of the land," the wonderful manna of YHWH "stopped."

The meaning "to rest" is also common. Beginning with the commandment to rest, the Bible refers to the demand often. A striking example may be found in another Exodus passage. At Exodus 23:10-11, generally considered to be a part of an old code of conduct, the command to rest is reiterated and a clear emphasis on the poor is given as the rationale. Also, the *day* of rest has now become a *year* of rest. "For six years you shall sow your land and gather in its yield, but the seventh year you shall let it rest and lie fallow, so that the poor of your people may eat; and what they leave the wild animals may eat. You shall do the same with your vineyard, and with your olive orchard." The command for equality in resting enshrined in the commandment has here become a claim that rest has a social purpose. We rest and the land rests in order that the poor and the wild creatures may eat! The implication is that constant labor without rest will exclude the poor and the wild creatures from the proceeds of that unceasing work. This connection between constant work and the exclusion of the poor and the animals has important implications for a culture like ours, which works more and more with the statistical result that a few get richer while the many get poorer. It may be that the demand that we rest is not merely a lovely opportunity for us to take a break from work; rest may be crucial if we are to order our community in the ways God has in mind.

SERMONIC NOTES (EXODUS)

1

Any sermon on the Exodus formulation of the fourth commandment will need to raise the question of the place of rest in the twenty-first century world of work. Any return to a "blue-law" world, where stores are shuttered, golf is banned, and yards remain unmowed, is fanciful and ludicrous. But as Exodus 23 suggests, there is a profound connection between our unwillingness to sanctify some time for rest and the safety and well-being of the poor, both human and animal. What can it possibly mean then for us to "sanctify" the Sabbath day?

As studies continue to show, we citizens of the United States are working longer and longer hours and are enjoying it less and less. Not only that, we are doing far less than we used to do when we worked fewer hours. We vacation less, we play less, we volunteer less, we join groups less frequently, we have less sex, we eat more fast food and grow less healthy. In short, we work more for less reward in human terms. The toll on our community is incalculably negative and dangerous. Exodus seems to be right; work without sanctified rest leads to community dissolution and inequalities of resources.

But what would "sanctified rest" look like? Here we must avoid falling back into a modern casuistry: *this* day, not *that* day; *this* way, not *that* way. Each believing person will need to determine the times and the ways she/he will sanctify a Sabbath. One thing is sure; the hour on Sunday morning may not be at all sufficient for a sanctified Sabbath. I would certainly urge all believers to join together in regular worship of God, but that worship in and of itself will not be enough sanctified rest to make an impact on the work-crazed world in which we live. Some of us may have to relearn how to play; some may have to learn how to be silent. The tasks will not be the same.

2

The issue of the countercultural justice of Sabbath-keeping is important. The Israelites are commanded to remember Sabbath by including all in their community in the celebration, from relatives, to slaves, to animals, to foreigners. The portrait of Sabbath memory here is little short of the great banquet promised by God upon the arrival of God's rule on earth and at the end of the age. Sabbath celebration is then nothing less than a prefiguring of God's realm, promised and coming. Surely, our segregated, single-classed, homogeneous Sunday morning services hardly resemble the Sabbath envisioned in the fourth commandment! A sermon focusing on the Lord's Supper and the fourth commandment as representations of the rule of God could help a congregation confront its insulation and isolation in a world of increasing diversity.

EXEGESIS OF THE FOURTH COMMANDMENT (DEUTERONOMY)

The introductory comments and subsequent history of the fourth commandment have been provided above, but there are some significant differences in the textual exegesis of Deuteronomy's formulation of the commandment.

1
"Keep/guard" (shamer)

This very common Hebrew word has a rather simple meaning; we are urged to protect something given to us, something already in existence that we did not create. Exodus commanded that we "remember the Sabbath" by *doing* what YHWH did: resting. Our "actions" of resting fulfill the commandment. Deuteronomy, on the other hand, commands that we "guard" the day, simply because YHWH has commanded it. Still, as in Exodus, we are to guard the day "by making it holy." We do that, says Exodus, by resting because YHWH rested. Not so for Deuteronomy.

Here we are commanded to rest for a very different reason. Rather than YHWH's creation rest, we are asked to remember not the Sabbath day itself, but that we were once slaves in Egypt, saved from our slavery by YHWH's powerful hand and outstretched arm. That is why we are to "make" Sabbath. Exodus says we make the day holy because YHWH made the day holy by the divine rest. Deuteronomy says we rest because we remember our historical past of slavery and remind ourselves that we are no longer slaves by our sanctified rest.

This emphasis on slavery is made clear by another difference Deuteronomy presents. The list of those who are commanded to rest is nearly the same as the one in Exodus, except that the general word "livestock" is made more specific with the addition of "oxen" and "donkey." But the important difference is the repetition of the words "male and female slaves." They are listed among those who are to rest, as in Exodus, but they conclude the clause as the very reason that the rest is commanded! It is exactly so that male and female slaves can rest that the commandment to rest is given at all!

This huge emphasis on the memory of Israel's slavery is of course central to the special concerns of Deuteronomy. The portrayal of Israel's slave origins stands at the heart of the theology of this book. Israel was in fact helpless and hopeless in the slaughterhouse of Egyptian bondage. If not for the love and power of YHWH, they would be there still. It is that memory that commands them to make the Sabbath holy and to celebrate it with all the community, most especially with the slaves who are a constant reminder of Israel's past. They must be allowed to rest, because

Israel does not want to be like the Egyptian taskmasters who treated them with such cruelty. Thus the Sabbath rest becomes the celebration that warns Israel that they must never become what their long-ago masters were.

SERMONIC NOTES (DEUTERONOMY)

Once again, a sermon could focus on the need for rest in a madly working world, but the emphasis for Deuteronomy is so clearly on the necessity of remembering the slave roots of Israel that a preacher should do some reflection on that point. This focus is really quite extraordinary. To be reminded of one's quite discredited and humiliating origins, to use that memory as a warning against becoming like those cruel masters who made one a slave, is a valuable way of avoiding what so often has happened in history: when the oppressed get the power, they become the oppressors. This fourth commandment in its Deuteronomy form shines as a beacon to those who would abuse power as if power were their God-given right.

Nearly all peoples have sprung from humble, if not disreputable, soil. Through luck and pluck and sometimes brains, great nations have formed. However, that "greatness" has often come on the backs of former "great" nations. This fourth commandment is one clear-eyed attempt to stop this terrible cycle of nation-building at the expense of others. I am reminded of the famous story of ancient Rome. Whenever a great victory was won for Rome, the conquering general was given a great "triumph," a victory parade through the city. However, always joining the general in his triumphal chariot was a tiny figure, often a slave, who was assigned one task. He was to whisper into the general's ear, again and again, in the midst of the cheering throngs, one phrase, *"Sic transit gloria mundi"*; roughly "the glory of the world does not last." There is little historical indication that this custom had much effect on the fortunes of Rome and its generals. So also it could be said that Deuteronomy's fourth commandment had little historical effect on the leaders of Israel who show the usual signs of greed (Solomon) and lust for sex and power (David) and corruption (Ahab) that other monarchs of other lands have regularly shown. Still, attention to the fourth commandment might prove salutary to any nation that thinks it always has been and always will be "king of the hill," and can use any other nations and peoples for its own purposes and desires. A Sabbath rest with attention to its real past, rather than an idealized one, could be very useful indeed. We citizens of the United States should know a nation like that rather well.

A sermon on the fourth commandment could directly address the vexed question of immigration to the United States. It is striking that both versions of the commandment admonish Israelites to include the foreigners living among them in the celebrations of Sabbath, most especially in the celebration of rest from work. In the United States it is often our immigrants, whether judged "legal or illegal," who do the vast portion of the work nobody else wants to do. It is said in my own city that if immigrants suddenly all decided to return home, at least three fourths of the city's restaurants would close for lack of workers.

I have returned recently from a trip to El Salvador. I learned there that the country's single greatest source of income is money sent back to the country from the one million Salvadoran immigrants living in the United States, some 1.5 billion dollars per year. Too often I hear the mantras of the fearful: "they take all our jobs"; "they use all of our welfare resources"; "they flood our schools with their own customs and languages, refusing to learn English." Israel was commanded to include their foreigners in their most important regular celebration, that of Sabbath. What would happen if we included the strangers among us, in all of their diversity, in our celebrations? What could we learn—about them and about ourselves? Perhaps we would be reminded that once we were strangers in a strange land, alone and basically friendless, trying to eke out a living while in rebellion against an established kingdom seen as oppressive. Perhaps we could say, in a paraphrase of a famous line from "Pogo," "We have met the immigrant and he/she is us."

CHAPTER FIVE

The Fifth Commandment

Honor your father and your mother so that your days will be long on the soil that YHWH your God is giving to you. (Exod. 20:12)

Honor your father and your mother just as YHWH your God commanded you so that your days may be long and so that it will be good for you on the soil that YHWH your God is giving to you. (Deut. 5:16)

Once again, as in the previous discussion, we find two versions of a commandment. Though the differences between the two versions here are not as striking as in the previous commandment, they do offer interesting possibilities to the preacher.

SUBSEQUENT HISTORY OF THE COMMANDMENT

The reformers, Luther and Calvin, both extracted a potentially dangerous meaning from this commandment. The former said that the commandment implied that one must not only honor parents, but must also love them. And since the word "honor" is only used in the presence of those who are "high and great,"[1] Luther moved to extend the commandment's meaning to include "various kinds of obedience due to our superiors, persons whose duty it is to command and to govern."[2] In other words, Luther claimed that because we are commanded to honor our fathers and mothers, we are also commanded to honor our superiors. I assume he means those in positions of authority, kings, governors, and teachers, among others. At least in Luther's own case, it is clear that this meaning of the commandment did not extend to the pope and his cardinals! Nevertheless, for Luther, the question of the legitimacy of the superior was an important one.

John Calvin made the same move as he approached the fifth commandment. It was given to us by God, he said, because mother and father represent all "on whom God has bestowed some excellence."[3] The importance of the commandment is thus not limited to the various ways we should go about honoring the leaders of our families. It admonishes us to show proper deference and love to those whom God has chosen to be our superiors. Calvin goes on to say, "It makes no difference whether our superiors are worthy or unworthy of this honor, for whatever they are they have attained their position through God's providence."[4] Once again, the pope in Rome would have been surprised, and no doubt quite pleased, if his rebellious sons, Luther and Calvin, had acted on their understanding of this commandment!

But the fact that they plainly did not so act with respect to the hierarchy of the Roman church, while leading to the Reformation, at the same time raised the vexed question of the power of secular and religious authority with new vigor. If all authority is of God (so Paul's claim in Romans 13:1), what is one to do in the face of a patently evil authority? When Luther was confronted with a peasant rebellion against the German authorities (nobles, including bishops and abbots) in 1524, a rebellion partly driven by the simplest desires for food and shelter, he urged a brutal repression of the rebels, after initially showing some sympathy with their cause. Indeed, he accused the rebels of being "mad dogs" who deserved whatever torture and death that the nobles could mete out. The nobles hardly needed much encouragement to act against the rebels with savagery.

In our own time, this question of honoring authorities is still with us. Those baby boomers who came to full consciousness in the 1960s well remember the outcries against the established authorities, driven by the Vietnam War, the Watergate episode which led to a presidential resignation, and the general notion that authority need not be followed merely because it is an authority. Those heirs of Luther and Calvin began to come to the conclusion that "honoring father and mother," as the prototype of honoring all authority, was inappropriate, a "sellout" to "the man," to an authority that had become evil and oppressive. "Love it or leave it," some traditional authorities shouted at those who called into question the United States' involvement in Vietnam; "change it or lose it," the rebels responded.

Though this reading of the fifth commandment has played an important role in the debate concerning the relationships people have with those who have authority over them, it has not been the only way that the fifth commandment has been heard. An equally important understanding of the commandment has focused more narrowly on the implications it has for family. Poteat suggests that its meaning is to "take your parents seriously—you may live a long time that way."[5] He expands the meaning of the word "honor" to include "serious." In this way, he tries to answer the question that surely must arise: *What if my mother and/or my father are not in any way worthy of my honor?* Poteat answers that one can take someone seriously even if they are dishonorable. However, this way of handling the commandment seems to me disingenuous. "To honor" certainly does assume a seriousness in the relationship, but the opposite is not the case; I can take someone very seriously without honoring that person at all—Adolf Hitler springs to mind. In the exegesis below, we will look more closely at the possible meanings of the word "honor."

Of course, in our day, "honoring father and mother" has become a cliché, albeit a rather meaningless one, I fear. It is a phrase often hurled around in a divorce trial, or is used, as a last resort, by a beleaguered parent when trying to coerce a recalcitrant child to behave. However, there is an important modern experience, known to increasing numbers of people, that has added a deep poignancy to the old commandment.

Recently, I received a phone call asking me if I would be willing to meet someone to talk about the meaning of the fifth commandment. A woman of late middle age came to my office the next day. She was having a problem that came directly from the way she had been trained to understand the fifth commandment. Her eighty-two-year-old mother was battling cancer, and then had suffered a stroke. Her daughter had come from another state to be with her mother in her recovery time—if there was to be a recovery. To make the situation even more difficult the daughter's husband had died of cancer less than two years before. She sat down, and immediately asked, "How can I honor my mother when I am having the very hardest time even liking her?" The mother-daughter relationship had never been very good, and now the constant demands on the daughter's time and energy were creating such powerful levels of resentment that the daughter wanted out of the situation. But she was deeply ashamed of that desire; she was certain that "to honor one's mother" was to be willing to provide for her unreservedly at least something of what her mother provided for the daughter when she was a baby.

I do not tell this story to offer an opportunity to evaluate my pastoral counseling skills! It is an example of an experience many are now having—the care of aging parents. My own wife cared for her mother for five years after a debilitating stroke, and felt many of the same things that the woman I talked with felt. I want to argue that care for aging parents is much closer to the original context for the fifth commandment than some demand that one's fifteen-year-old behave. Understanding the biblical context of the commandment should make this special relevance clear.

EXEGESIS OF THE FIFTH COMMANDMENT

1
"Honor" (kabod)

The basic meaning of the word is "heaviness" in the physical sense, as well as "gravity" and "importance" in the metaphorical sense. This movement of meaning leads to "honor" and "respect." Hebrew offers a perfect antonym to the word: *qalal*, "lightness" in the physical sense, leading to "slightness" or "insignificance" or even "contempt" in the metaphorical sense. YHWH warns the old priest, Eli, that because of his rebellious sons, the days of Eli's priesthood are over. "Far be it from me! Surely, whoever honors *(kabod)* me, I will honor, but whoever despises me, I treat as contemptible *(qalal)*" (1 Sam. 2:30). The same contrast between honor and contempt is found in 2 Samuel 6:22 where David rejects the mockery of his wife, Michal, who scorns his dancing before the ark as vulgar. "I will make myself even more contemptible *(qalal)* than this—but by your maids, I will be held in honor *(kabod)*." Isaiah, in an oracle against the nation of Tyre, plays on the same contrasting words (23:9).

Though it is usually God who receives honor (Pss. 24:7, 9, 10; 29:3; 145:11; Jer. 2:11), it is also said that parents and slavemasters should receive it, too. Malachi 1:6 reads, "A son should honor his father and a slave his master," but even there it is God who is finally most worthy of honor. In the literature of wisdom, especially in the Proverbs, *kabod* can denote personal honor and dignity. Such honor can be gained by proper conduct—restraint and generosity—or by the proper character traits like humility (see Prov. 20:3; 11:16; 15:33). It is clear that the demand that we honor God must be seen as an analogy to the command that we honor parents.

But just who are these parents? Harrelson is surely correct when he says, "We believe that this commandment, like the others, has the adult members of the community clearly and prominently in view. . . . The commandment focused on the treatment of aged parents by the mature members of the community."[6] Certainly one of the earliest extended commentaries on the fifth commandment from Ben Sirach (Ecclesiasticus) of the second century B.C.E. makes this fact very likely. In Sirach's third chapter, he gives extended advice about the appropriate ways a son or daughter should honor his/her mother and father. For example, "Whoever honors his father atones for sins, and whoever glorifies his mother is like one who lays up treasure" (Sirach 3:3 RSV). Verses 12-13 provide the context of these admonitions: "O son, help your father in his old age, and do not grieve him as long as he lives; even if he is lacking in understanding, show forbearance; in all your strength do not despise him. For kindness to a father will not be forgotten" (RSV). And of course there is a very practical outcome for those who do honor their aged parents: "Whoever honors his father will be gladdened by his own children" (3:5 RSV). Our children learn much from watching us deal with our aging parents. What we hope they learn is helpful ways to deal with us as we age.

Thus, Sirach's ancient commentary points us to the appropriate context for an understanding of the fifth commandment. Yet, two other phrases are important as we attempt a fuller hearing.

2
"So that your days may be long"

The immediate consequence of a true honoring of one's aging parent is a long life. How is that to be understood? Surely, there is no thought of an automatic assurance of fine old age if one treats one's parents well. The Hebrews knew as well as we know that there is no such mechanical system in place in God's universe; many who deeply honor their parents die too soon, and many who treat their parents with contempt live long and seemingly happy lives. To believe such a thing is to run the risk of creating enormous guilt and shame in those who would try to understand their lives as a series of events based solely on their adherence to a list of immutable laws of behavior.

Right behavior is never an assurance of long life and success, as any reasonable human being knows too well. Again, Harrelson directs us correctly: the commandment "calls upon every human being to refrain from any action that would denigrate the life and worth of human beings who have lost much of their 'commercial' worth, and in particular those human beings on whom one's own life has depended."[7] Long life cannot be assured, but honoring those who have lived long provides a model for those who are younger, thus making the possibility of a fruitful continuity of caring more likely. Childs puts it this way: honoring "parental authority is integral to the divine order of blessing."[8] He notes Proverbs 1:8, 15:5, and especially 19:26 as places where proper honoring of parents is constitutive of the continuing success and fruitfulness of the godly community. On the contrary, to curse father and mother leads quite literally to death, according to Exodus 21:15, 17 and Leviticus 20:9. To show honor and respect to one's parents makes possible a long life, both for the individual and for the community that prizes such behavior.

3
"On the soil" ('adhamah)

This is an important formulation. It is true that the Hebrew *'adhamah* is often used as a synonym with the more common word "land, country" *(eretz)*. But the more earthy "soil" connects the commandment to the long tradition of Israel's history of election by YHWH. Israel owes its ancestral land only to YHWH. Over and over again, readers are reminded that without YHWH's gift there would be no land for the people. YHWH swore to the ancestors of Israel to give them the *'adhamah* both as a place to live and as a basis for their existence.[9]

However, there is a theological change in the conception of the gift of the land from the older notion of pure gift (Num. 11:12; 32:11) to the notion that the gift was in reality a conditional one. This change obviously occurred in the light of what was happening in Israel's history: the land was in fact lost. First, late in the eighth century B.C.E., the northern kingdom of Israel was decimated by the Assyrians, and then in the sixth century, the Judean community was destroyed by the Babylonians. The gift of the land could thus no longer be considered a perpetual one; its maintenance as Israel's land was increasingly seen as the result of right behavior. This is true even in light of Deuteronomy's conviction that YHWH intends to give the land to Israel "forever" (Deut. 4:40). That "forever" is clearly conditioned by behavioral requirements centering around following "all the commandments" that YHWH has commanded (31:13).

The promise to honor one's parents, leading to long life on the soil, is matched by the demand that one possess and use only honest weights and measures (Deut. 25:13-16)! Such honesty in commercial transactions leads to "many days on the soil" no less than the honoring of parents. This identical formulation provides an important clue to a fuller meaning of the fifth commandment. Deuteronomy 25:16 warns: "All who do such things (use dishonest scales—see Amos 8:5-6 for an eighth century example of such behavior), all who act dishonestly, are an abomination to YHWH." The word translated "abomination" is among the strongest terms used in cultic and ritual contexts to express YHWH's extreme repugnance at human behaviors. Actions such as idolatry, the sacrifice of one's own children, various forms of unchaste sexual activities, certain kinds of improper food, are all included under the rubric of "abomination to YHWH." No less is the dishonest use of weights and measures seen as an abomination, the result of which will be few days on the soil.

In the same way, not to honor one's parents will likewise lead to few days on the soil given by YHWH. But even more, not to honor one's parents is by analogy an abomination to YHWH. No less than idolatry and child sacrifice, so also is the refusal to honor parents repugnant to the giver of the soil.

EXEGESIS OF THE FIFTH COMMANDMENT (DEUTERONOMY)

There are two additions to Deuteronomy's formulation of the fifth commandment.

1
"Just as YHWH your God commanded you"

This phrase is one of the hallmarks of the style of the Deuteronomistic historian, examples of which may be seen from Deuteronomy, Kings, and Jeremiah. For Deuteronomy, the key to long life and success is to follow the direct commands of YHWH, revealed to Israel most especially through the mouth of YHWH's greatest prophet, Moses. The entire book of Deuteronomy is constructed as a series of sermons, given by Moses to an Israel on the verge of entering the land long promised. The central claim of each of the sermons is that YHWH has given clear guidelines for the emerging community. To follow those guidelines is to guarantee long life; to reject the guidelines leads to disaster. Because the final formulation of Deuteronomy was certainly after the exile of Israel to Babylon in the sixth century B.C.E., the authors had history on the side of their theology; Israel had obviously not followed the commands of YHWH and had thus lost the long-promised land.

It is not difficult to see the dangerous consequences of such a theological formulation. First, one could begin to believe that all occurrences are the direct result of whether or not certain rules have been followed in certain ways. To cite two contemporary and unfortunate examples: (1) a huge tornado destroyed major sections of a Texas city some years ago, and several preachers in the city were quoted as saying that God was using the great storm to warn the people of that city that they needed to stop their wicked ways; (2) a jetliner crashed last year, killing the majority of the passengers, but one of the few survivors attributed his rescue to the fact that he was reading his Bible as the plane plunged to earth. These two claims sound nothing less than magical in their certainty that following the proper rules or prescribed religious behaviors will lead inevitably to desired results. Such magical claims are tragically present in many cancer wards where proper prayer, correct beliefs, are enjoined on sufferers in order to effect the needed cure. If the cure is not forthcoming, the faith was somehow inadequate.

The book of Job, among its many gifts to believers, is designed to call such magical claims into the most serious question. The supremely righteous Job receives nothing but disaster from a God he expected to act in the magical ways illustrated above. What he learns, and what all believers must learn, is that God simply is not a heavenly vending machine, passing out favors to those who put in the right amount of religious change. And that leads to the second danger of such a belief, which is far the more important one.

To believe that human behavior determines precisely what God will do is to reduce God to little more than the chief of the heavenly police force. Break the law; pay the consequences. Do the crime; do the time! Such a mechanical view of God reduces the life of faith to a list of actions prescribed and proscribed: do this, don't do that. And it reduces God to an adjunct to our actions. Such a God is bound to our behaviors, and is not free to be the God Israel affirmed God to be, that mysterious, radically free Holy One, who chose them out of love, who gave them the soil as a place for a great experiment of a just community, and who again and again wooed them to return to God's desired rule over their lives.

No use of the fifth commandment can suggest that honoring parents will inevitably lead to many days on the soil. Nor can any use of the fifth commandment suggest that "following the strict command of YHWH" will inevitably lead to "good for you."

2
"That it will be good for you"

This second addition to Deuteronomy's formulation of the fifth commandment, like the first, is typical Deuteronomic language. The phrase, at least on the surface, sounds quite innocuous. Honor your father and mother, and "it will be good for you." The phrase is so vague as to appear to have little real meaning. Yet, wrapped up in the tiny word "good" *(tob)*, are some important considerations.

This simple word is used hundreds of times in the Hebrew Bible, and has the basic meaning of "benefit" or "a pleasing thing." From that meaning arises notions of "welfare, prosperity, happiness." Individuals are regularly called "good" when they are prosperous and happy, sometimes leading to the unfortunate conclusion that "goodness" leads to "prosperity," the dangers of which were discussed above. Still, saying that the search for good, as opposed to the desire for evil, is YHWH's command may summarize much of the Bible's wisdom tradition (Proverbs in particular). Clearly, to honor father and mother is to do a "good" thing which itself will lead to good.

SERMONIC NOTES

1

Any sermon on the fifth commandment will want to deal with the question of the central relationship within families: that between parent and child, between child and parent. It cannot be denied that all human relationships, for good or ill, develop in association with those relationships that emerge in families. One need not be a follower of Freud or Jung, be acquainted with the latest techniques of family and relationship therapies, or be a skilled pastoral counselor, to know that our abilities to relate one to the other are honed—or not honed—in the crucibles of our families. How my parents treated me will have a profound effect on the ways I treat my significant relationships now.

A sermon that enters into the sometimes murky waters of family relationships, especially exploring the role of the honoring of parents, should be concerned to illustrate those relationships from the biblical record. Fortunately, the Bible is filled with superb examples of the ways parent-child contacts affect later relationships. The wonderful story of Joseph and his brothers comes to mind.

Jacob's favoritism toward his youngest son, Joseph (learned by him from his own father, Isaac!), leads Joseph to a complex relationship with his brothers and with his aging father, Jacob. After the brothers' failed attempt to murder Joseph, and after they are forced to come to Egypt in search of food, Joseph, now Secretary of Agriculture over all Egypt, recognizes them immediately but treats them as spies (Gen. 42). In the succeeding three chapters he plays a cruel cat and mouse game with them, lying again and again about their money, their grain, and a special cup he plants in the sack of Benjamin, the new youngest son of Jacob. During all this chicanery, Joseph does two unusual things. First, he weeps silently three times as if privately knowing that the tricks he is playing on the unsuspecting brothers really are cruel and unusual punishment for their earlier sin against him. Second, he asks three times about the health of his father, Jacob, by asking "Is the old man still alive?" Does the form of this question imply that he is genuinely concerned about Jacob's health, or is it a nasty way of probing whether or not the old man is surviving the games of the master puppeteer that Joseph has become? After all, who better than Joseph could know what the loss of the old man's favorite would do to him, as he, Joseph, the original favorite, demands that Benjamin be brought to Egypt before he will grant the food requests of the brothers? Family difficulties do not end when Joseph grandly reveals his true identity to the astounded brothers. After the death of the father, the brothers are still so terrorized by their all-powerful brother that they use their dead father in a lie in order to escape what they are sure will be the murderous revenge of Joseph against them (Gen. 50).

One could hardly discover a more potent example of the enormous effects generated by the ways parents and children relate to one another. Surely, a helpful discussion of the rich meanings of the word "honor" might go a long way toward redeeming the tangled family mess that the story of Joseph and his father and brothers demonstrates. It might help in the tangled messes that our families often find themselves in, too.

2

Walter Harrelson provides a wider lens within which one can view the fifth commandment.

> The only reality within the family—certainly Israel's central social institution—that requires attention within the Decalogue is the relation between parent and child, between child and parent. ... And if there is real health in the relation of adult parents to their elderly parents, there will be health in the other relations of the family. For it is how one deals with the helpless, with those who can no longer fend for themselves, and with such helpless ones against whom one has a lifetime

of grievances for wrongs done or imagined, that provides the test of one's moral and human commitments. ... those who show contempt for the poor, the orphan, and the widow will treat their elderly parents with contempt, and vice versa.[10]

Harrelson has opened the commandment up to the prophetic tradition with this insight. In the same way that the nation of Israel was said to be responsible for the weak ones among them, characterized by the group "stranger, widow, orphan," so care for elderly parents is a further sign of God's call for such responsibility. There is no doubt that our nation's elderly care facilities are among the loneliest places on the planet, stocked with persons whom time and families have too often forgotten. Our relationships with our aging parents are nothing less than laboratories for testing our larger commitments to the "least of these." Jesus' famous story from Matthew 25 concerning judgment for human activities concludes with that tiny yet powerful clause, "the least of these." It is finally our treatment of these persons that will lead to acceptance, or not, into the coming rule of God. In this light, the fifth commandment is lifted out of an individual commandment concerning the way I should treat my aging parents; it becomes a sign of my commitment to the "wretched of the earth," a signal announcing whether I will answer the prophetic call to "serve God and my neighbor in all that I do."

3

If a preacher were interested in making some connections between the first five commandments, the ones often named "theological," as opposed to the last five, sometimes called "social," the following comments will prove helpful. (As we continue our discussion of the commandments, it may prove less helpful to divide and define the commandments in these broad ways.) The first five commandments announce realities without which no community would survive for long. Communities that engage in various forms of idolatry, who treat YHWH as nonexistent or nonsignificant, who define themselves by their constant work and never rest, who forget their responsibilities to their elderly parents, hence to the "least of these," are communities doomed to pass away. The first five commandments aim for what Harrelson calls, "overall compliance by the community."[11] Unless a community continues to push for all of its members' adherence to these first five commandments, the very structure of the community itself is deeply threatened. Harrelson goes on to suggest that the next five commandments have more to do with individual acts which will always, unfortunately, be perpetrated by members of every community. However, those individual aberrations do not in themselves threaten the destruction of the entire community. But if communities do not have at their very core the convictions enshrined in commandments one through five, they will implode or will fly apart, lacking a central conviction, a basic glue that will enable them to cohere.[12]

A sermon with this concern will want to ask about the basic convictions of a community; just what is the central core of the nation, of the church, of groups within the church? What is the beating heart of this particular assembly of people? The clear answer of the first commandment is the call to center ourselves in the God who brought us up from the slaughterhouse of Egypt, out of the house of slavery, and who lures us away from all the slaveries we continually find so attractive to us. It is only in this unique and particular God that a community of faith can find its true anchor.

CHAPTER SIX

The Sixth Commandment

You must not kill.

Certainly no two Hebrew words have generated more commentary, both richly informed and dangerously ill-informed, than the two words of the sixth commandment—*lo tirtsach*. I have translated "you must not" to suggest the urgency and passion with which the commandment is infused. In effect, this is more than a simple prohibition; it is a passionate urging to avoid the act of killing, seemingly at all costs.

But therein lies one of the greatest problems with this commandment. How can one imagine that it commends an absolute avoidance of all killing when the Hebrew Bible is filled with killing of many kinds, some of it sanctioned both by the community and by YHWH? It is quite clear that the Hebrew Scriptures appear to sanction both capital punishment (see Deut. 24:16 for one example among many) and war (see 1 Sam. 15:2-3, for example, a demand from YHWH, through the mouth of Samuel, to stage an annihilating preemptive strike against Amalek). It is this apparent contradiction between command and practice that has led to a welter of opinion concerning the "real" meaning of the sixth commandment.

Hauerwas and Willimon give a clear statement of what readers of this commandment are *not* allowed to do.

> In our attempts to weasel out of this command, we shall not be helped much by saying, "It doesn't really mean kill; it means murder." The Hebrew verb "to kill" does mean "murder" in

certain contexts (cf. 1 Kings 21:9), but it can also refer to unintentional killing (Deut. 4:41-42), as well as execution of a duly
convicted killer (Num. 35:30).[1]

It has often been said that the command itself was restricted
to what we moderns call "murder" precisely because war and
capital punishment were features of ancient Israelite culture.
But the linguistic evidence will not sustain such a reading. The
verb, one of several verbs for killing used in the Hebrew Bible,
has a very broad use. Therefore, its use in the sixth commandment cannot be a restricted one. And because that is true, the
very real danger arises that the commandment may finally have
no significant meaning at all. After all, if we are warned against
killing of all sorts here, while killing of all sorts occurs elsewhere, and is even sanctioned elsewhere, the force of the commandment is seriously undercut.

And if that danger was alive for the Israelites, it is certainly alive
for us modern Christians. However much we may piously recite
"You must not kill," our culture is without doubt the most overtly
violent in all of recorded history. During a recent calendar year in
the United States, more than thirty-five thousand deaths by
firearms were recorded and nearly the same number were killed in
traffic accidents. Added together, these two figures exceed the total
number of American deaths in all of the Vietnam War. And, as we
have already noted, the twentieth century was the most fantastically bloody one hundred years in all of history with a nearly incal-
culable number of deaths and wounded casualties in two world
wars and numerous smaller conflicts, unfortunately not "smaller"
in terms of casualties. What possible significance could this quite
absurd two-word command have in the face of this mountain of
maimed and dead humanity?

I want to suggest two responses to that gnawing question. First,
as I have tried to say earlier, it is crucial that we not separate this
commandment from the ones that have preceded it. As the sixth
commandment has most directly stated, despite the actual evidence provided in other biblical instances, human life is to be protected from all acts of violence that threaten the "continued
existence of life itself."[2] The first commandment expressed the
basic truth about YHWH's relationship to the whole of life when it
claims that YHWH is the one who brought us out of our slavery,

and the second commandment demanded that we offer unqualified allegiance to that God who has authority over all life. Thus, when we are commanded, "You must not kill," we are warned that any human killing is far from routine; it can never become some ordinary outcome of a legally constituted system of justice nor some inevitable result of a declaration of war, however justified such a war may claim to be. Because all life is in fact God's life, we humans take life at our peril. No killing can ever be a cause for rejoicing. Weeping may be the appropriate response whenever killing is done, no matter the circumstances.

The second response to the apparent absurdity of the sixth commandment is well stated by Hauerwas and Willimon. "Rather than ponder how we might skillfully reinterpret this command to suit present circumstances, our time might be better spent wondering how we might change the church to be the sort of place that produces and supports nonviolent people."[3] It is little less than shocking that a church, founded in the name of one known as the "Prince of Peace," continues to exist, and often to thrive, in the very heart of this ultraviolent culture. Where are the voices of the church raised in protest of this violence? Isolated peacemakers aside (Martin Luther King, Jr., Daniel Berrigan, Jim Wallis, among others), the church has too often either stood silent in the face of violence or has, more terribly, supported violence in the name of some supposed theological principle.

I live in Texas, where more people have been executed at the request of the state over the past year than in any other year since the reinstatement of the death penalty in the 1970s. As these persons are killed, outside the prison walls, loud parties are led by church people, celebrating the ending of life in the places of execution. What have these persons' churches taught them about God and God's authority over all life and all death? Why are they so glad to see a life end, a life given by God? Is this killing the stuff of celebration? What roles do our churches play in the cult of violence that seems to sweep our land?

THE SUBSEQUENT HISTORY OF THE SIXTH COMMANDMENT

Luther's Large Catechism sets the tone for much of the later understanding and complex use of the sixth commandment. The reformer claimed that this commandment prohibits killing by private individuals, but does not abrogate that right for governments. This is true since parents had to bring their children into judgment and had even to sentence them to death (quoting the terrible Deut. 21:18-20). As we saw in Luther's earlier discussion of the previous commandment concerning honor due to parents, those in authority had power over their charges. And because parents had that enormous authority, even over the life and death of their children, so too did governments, as God's rightly constituted authorities, have that authority over their people.

Luther also extends the meaning of the commandment to include a prohibition of anger against others. But again the exception is "persons who occupy the place of God, that is, parents and rulers."[4] Anger, he thought, can lead to dangerous acts and can thereby be a deep threat to the tranquillity of a community. However, legally constituted anger, that of parents against recalcitrant children, and rulers against recalcitrant subjects, is appropriate and is thus of God.

But Luther's extension of the commandment goes further. The commandment against killing also implies that deeds *not* done can also in effect be murderous. Luther notes Matthew 25 and its warning against those who refuse to serve "the least of these," suggesting that refusal to aid can itself be killing. He claims that a refusal to clothe a naked person is just like a refusal to save a drowning person; both cases are cases of murder.[5]

But in still another extension of meaning, Luther reminds his readers that, because of the first commandment, all who would truly follow the commandments need to "subdue our desire for revenge."[6] The first commandment makes it clear that only God has ultimate power and authority, not any human being. Our desire for revenge must necessarily be curbed in the light of that fact.

Thus, Luther's extensions are three, and are matched by later commentators. He claims that the sixth commandment prohibits personal anger, warns us that omitted actions can be fully as murderous as overt killing, and that personal revenge, a revenge that could lead to further mayhem, is to be avoided in the light of the ultimate authority of God. These three extensions nicely mirror the ecclesial schizophrenia demonstrated throughout the subsequent use and abuse of the sixth commandment.

Preachers have long inveighed against personal anger that leads to violence and destruction of the communities of family and neighborhood. And preachers have long warned their hearers that failure to act individually can be as deadly as acting in anger or revenge. Yet, like Luther, preachers have been too often unwilling to extend these statements against anger and revenge to a national level, and have not done so for reasons similar to Luther's, albeit using different language than his. While he would say that rulers (and parents) have authority given to them by God, we might say that governments have authority because they are legally elected. And that legal status demands that we who elected them are responsible to follow their dictates. If the law allows capital punishment, we are duty bound to perform it when the law says it is appropriate. When the state declares a war, we are duty bound to support that war with our material goods and our physical service.

However, if the commandment suggests that violence itself is the problem, and that the power over life and death is God's and not ours, both our personal desire for violence and the state's desire to condone violence may be called into question by the higher authority of God. We will return to this discussion in the sermon notes below.

Extensions of the sixth commandment in the manner of Luther are legion. R. H. Charles claims that the sale of alcohol breaks the sixth commandment (since it so often leads to mayhem and death), as does poor housing construction, overpopulation (lack of proper controls), overwork, bad working conditions, and so forth.[7] Indeed, for Charles, anything at all that could possibly lead to injury or death is rejected by this commandment. This is a classic case of extending the meaning of a commandment so far as to make its meaning well-nigh meaningless! Edwin Poteat says that because "man is not an end in himself," that is, is not the final goal of creation, the prohibition against killing in this commandment is absolute. He believes that the story of the murder of Abel by Cain is a biblical rejection of the right of humans to take the life of other humans. Poteat thus, unlike Luther, rejects both war and capital punishment as a "destruction of the Creator's will." "To kill a man is a confession that nothing else can be done with him."[8]

Clovis Chappell says that in the sixth commandment "we are forbidden to take life directly," as the murder of Abel makes clear.[9] Suicide is likewise rejected, as is the taking of "needless physical risks," and the waging of war. What this commandment implies is "active life-giving." This is made certain when Jesus in his Matthean list of contraries (Matt. 5:21-22) extends the meaning of the sixth commandment to include anger, in effect making unrestrained anger equal to killing.

As we can see, the extensions of the meaning of the sixth commandment are many and various but revolve around the issues of the state's role in killing, primarily war and capital punishment, and the necessity or not of our active participation in the building-up of life rather than the taking of it. Perhaps a closer exegesis of the command can provide further clues to its possible meanings in our time.

EXEGESIS OF THE SIXTH COMMANDMENT

At one level, we need only exegete the single verb of the command. The verb *ratsach* is relatively rare, its use concentrated in a few places only in the Hebrew Bible. For example, Numbers 35 presents fourteen instances of the word (of a total of fewer than forty). The complex rules regarding killing, both intentional and unintentional, enshrined in Numbers 35 are a window to the emerging questions of a community wrestling with the various issues of killing. In the chapter, the *rotsa'ach*, the unintentional killer, is allowed to flee from immediate revenge to one of the cities of refuge, places designated for safety from "the redeemer of blood (*go'el*)," the designated avenger of a wrongful death. If the killer acted accidentally and without hatred, he (and presumably she) had the right to escape retribution by hiding in the city of refuge. He/she was then required to remain there while the current High Priest of the community remained alive. If the killer stepped out of the city of refuge, he/she was fair game for the retribution of the redeemer of blood. However, intentional killers (*rotsa'ach*—the same word is used) had by necessity to be put to death. No ransom, whether monetary or personal, can be provided for the murderer by intent; they must die, because the land is polluted by the innocent blood that has been shed. Only the blood of the one who shed the blood of another can expiate for the polluted land (v. 33). The fact that the same word is used here for the intentional and unintentional killer makes clear that the sixth commandment cannot be translated "you must not murder." The prescription is against killing, not murder only.

The prescription for these cities of refuge is also discussed several times in Deuteronomy (4:42; 19:3, 4, 6) and in Joshua (20:3, 5, 6; 21:13, 21, 27, 32, 38). However, though all of these Deuteronomic references refer only to unintentional killing, that is hardly the case at 1 Kings 21:19. There Ahab's secondhand murder of Naboth in order to steal his vineyard is termed by Elijah to be nothing other than a brutal killing, using the familiar word. And Job, during a lengthy description of the earth's cruelties, describes "the murderer *(rotsa'ach)* who arises at dusk to kill the poor and needy, and in the night is like a thief" (Job 24:14 NRSV). Furthermore, Hosea adds an interesting twist to the meaning of the word, when he charges the priests of his day with "murder on the road to Shechem," no better than thieves lying in wait (Hos. 6:9). Because Hosea has just announced in verse 6 that God "desire[s] steadfast love and not sacrifice, the knowledge of God rather than burnt offerings" (NRSV), the "murder" that the priests commit is apparently their refusal to engage in deeds of justice rather than empty sacrificial practices (see also Amos 5:21-24).

Thus, we may conclude that the language of the sixth commandment includes all sorts of killing, intentional and unintentional, hate-filled and innocent. We are led to conclude that the commandment urges us to live a life without killing. Are there other places in the tradition that might suggest such a life?

Genesis 1 enshrines many foundational ideas in its remarkable poetry, but one that is not often emphasized is the call for a life without killing. "Look," says God, "I have given to you every plant yielding seed that is upon the surface of the whole earth, as well as every tree with seed inside its fruit; you shall have them for food" (Gen. 1:29 NRSV). And this vegetarian lifestyle is also demanded for the animals (Gen. 1:30)! Of course, the Hebrews were not fools; they knew quite well that many of the animals, not to mention themselves, were hardly vegetarians. But in their ensuing telling of the primeval story, they described how disordered their world had become, a world far from the intention of the Creator.

First came the disobedience of fruit-eating (Gen. 3), followed by the horror of fratricide (Gen. 4). Then the enormous deluge came, brought on by the fantastic and unending evil of the human creation (Gen. 6:5). From these appalling reprobates, God chose to save one family, whose function was to bring rest to the ground from which humans were taken (Gen. 5:29). But after the flood dried up, the family's patriarch drank excessively from his vineyard, lay naked in his tent, and destroyed and scattered the saved family throughout the earth. But before that disaster, God covenanted with Noah, giving to him the restored earth. However, things were hardly the same in this post-flood land. Now, meat-eating was allowed (Gen. 9:2-4), and words like "fear" and "dread" now signified the relationship between God's human and animal creations. Likewise, human beings will now shed one another's blood to "make a reckoning" for shed blood. Though many have used these lines to provide biblical proof that God "demands" a blood reckoning, requires capital punishment, it should be remembered that the eating of meat—hence the death of some that others may live—and the existence of capital punishment occurs only in a post-flood world. It is not in the world that God intended that such things should happen; Genesis 1 is not Genesis 9; human sin has occurred in an avalanche between these chapters. Only in a fallen world will meat be eaten and capital punishment occur.

Hence, a world of nonviolence, unknown to the Hebrews and largely unknown to us, could be said to be the world desired by God. The sixth commandment is given as a counterpoint to a mad world, bent on destruction of one another, and ultimately on self-destruction. As Hauerwas and Willimon have it: "Christians are not simply prohibited from killing, but also invited to live in a way that does not force us to kill." [10]

Perhaps the finest portrayal of such a possible life comes in this unforgettable passage from Isaiah:

> The wolf shall live with the lamb,
>   the leopard shall lounge with the goat,
> the calf and the lion and the sacrificial animals together,
>   and a tiny child shall lead them all.

The cow and the bear shall graze,
   their young shall lie down together;
   and the lion shall eat straw like the ox.
The nursing child shall play in the snake's hole,
   while the older child shall puts its hand in the puff
     adder's den.
They will not hurt or destroy on all my holy mountain,
for the earth will be filled with YHWH's knowledge
   just as the waters cover the sea. (Isa. 11:6-9)

Here is God's desire for God's nonviolent world. Carnivores become herbivores; poisoners become playmates; children become leaders; warriors give up their war and play happily with their supposed enemies. Such absurd dreams! Such make-believe foolishness! Such a world far from the one we know all too well. But we must never forget the proverb: "Where there is no envisioning, the people die" (Prov. 29:18). Unless we keep the greatest hopes of God before us, we doom ourselves to a life of no abundance, a life hardly worth the living.

SERMONIC NOTES

Any sermon on the sixth commandment needs to avoid a discussion of legalistic requirements that are said to follow from a proper reading of the commandment. Questions like: Should Christians go to war? or Can Christians support capital punishment?, while continually interesting (and continually designed to get preachers into hot water!), are not the most basic questions to be raised in a discussion of this commandment. If the command is seen as another countercultural one, not unlike the command for Sabbath observance, the sermon will want to address the culture of violence against which this command is directed. It may indeed be necessary in this post-flood world to go to war. It may indeed be necessary in this post-flood world to practice capital punishment in the most extreme cases. However, whether or not a Christian is to participate in either of those two practices cannot be decided on the strength of a reading of the sixth commandment alone.

It seems clear that a countercultural reading of the commandment could just as easily lead to the notion that any war, however justified it appears to be, is against the nonviolent world envisioned by a God who claims vengeance and retribution only for Godself. Such a reading could also lead to the thought that capital punishment is nothing less than usurping God's final authority to rule over life and death, and that to put anyone to death, however monstrous that person appears to be, is to claim that we are God, determining finally who will live and who will die. And further, by participating in this ultimate punishment, we say that God has no power to redeem even the hardest of hearts, to find life and hope where there seems to be only death and evil. Such notions may be viewed as little more than cloudlike fantasies, ephemeral foolishness for the permanently idiotic. We live in the real world of real evil, real injustice, and real cruelty. We must combat these forces, not act as if they do not exist! Still, I wonder. Is there not "a more excellent way," as Paul's famous chapter has it (1 Cor. 13)? Is not the love that is never boastful or rude, that outlasts all religious speech and sparkling good deeds, that goes beyond even martyrdom itself, finally what does abide? Is such a countercultural, nonviolent love so silly after all? Or is it the way of God?

At the same time that the preacher may want to address the new vision of a nonviolent world that the sixth commandment may point us to, she/he may need to correct the sometimes fanciful notions extant surrounding the meanings of the commandment. One could call this work, "clearing the decks." In fact, any sermon that attempts to discuss the Ten Commandments will need to reckon carefully with the myriad of ideas floating around the famous Ten. Can the sixth commandment be translated "you must not murder"? We have seen that the answer is plainly, no. And the implications of why the answer is no will need to be addressed. Is the proper meaning of the commandment that all life is inherently sacred and hence should be preserved? Is the killing of mosquitoes to be avoided as a shattering of the sixth commandment? Again, I think the answer is no, but the reasons for the answer, primarily that it is God who is finally the sacred one, need to be discussed. Can an abortion foe merely quote this commandment to seal his or her victory against an abortion proponent? Can an antigun person simply quote the commandment to defeat a member of the NRA in oral combat? The answers to both question are again, no. But reasons within the Ten Commandments themselves and within the broader traditions of the Bible will need to be adduced to demonstrate why that is so.

The work of "deck-clearing" is crucial before a new idea can be presented. If the preacher does not clear the decks, it is nearly certain that the hearers will preach their own sermons, finding fulfillment for what they already believe about this commandment, or outright rejecting any idea that does not affirm what they already believe.

A sermon could take on directly those passages that are often quoted to prove a given point of view. For example, proponents of capital punishment regularly point to Genesis 9:5–6 as a proof text for their convictions. As I suggested above in the exegesis section, a rather different way to read the entire primeval history (Gen. 1–11) can be followed to offer a counterdiscussion to the familiar one. If Genesis 9 is not a command of God, but a recognition of the evil world in which we now live, capital punishment may be seen as a horrid fact in a fallen world and not a requirement given by God. The response to that fact is not joy, but sorrow, not celebration, but a deep sadness that once again we have given testimony that we do not live in a world desired by the Creator, but rather a world of our own cruel design. However, while one makes such an argument, it should be made clear that a simple quotation of the sixth commandment is not sufficient proof that capital punishment is wrong.

A sermon on the sixth commandment could attempt to describe just what a life given over to life-fulfilling rather than life-taking would look like. How could a Christian live in a violent world in a nonviolent way? What would be the risks of such a life? What would be the joys? Is vegetarianism a proper response toward such a life? Are all called to be vegetarian? Can a Christian refuse to participate in any war and thereby fulfill one reading of the sixth commandment? A preacher will need to think long and deeply about this new way of thinking about life so as to avoid a new legalism, a new list of rules by which one can be somehow assured of a nonviolent life in a violent world. A different sort of self-righteousness could be the result of such shallow reflection. How could one make the vision of Isaiah 11 any sort of reality? Or is that finally just "pie-in-the-sky"?

CHAPTER SEVEN

The Seventh Commandment

You must not commit adultery.

Once again, we have two small words fraught with enormous power, words that have had the most significant and dangerous consequences throughout the history of their use. The definition of the word in English is clear enough: sexual intercourse between a married person, either man or woman, and another who is not that person's spouse. Though the word has come to possess that meaning in the modern era, its biblical connotation was rather different, as we shall see.

We live in a culture that is little less than notorious for disregarding the seventh commandment. In fact, many discussions of this commandment generally turn to sniggering and bad jokes. It is astonishing how much of network TV is based on flagrant adultery between consenting, hot-blooded "adults." There is a remarkable irony in naming this activity *"adultery"* since so much of the behavior appears to be more juvenile than adult. How easy it would be, in the face of the promiscuity so evident among us, to become righteously indignant and to return to the strict punishments for such activities prescribed in the Bible. Death by public stoning, for example! Tragically, in Afghanistan under the Taliban, the most strictly Islamic nation in modern times, a woman caught in the act of adultery was stoned to death in an outdoor stadium with thousands of people as witnesses. Her execution was seen as a public warning against any others who would engage in such depraved behavior.

But is this public horror on the one hand, and a sly wink and a shrug on the other, the only two options available to the preacher who would address this question? I want to suggest a third possibility. Nearly seven years ago, I was appointed as the interim minister of a large church whose pastor had been accused of sexual harassment by several women on the staff of the church, and eventually by many more women. The accusations ranged from verbal abuse to sexual intercourse. During my four months there, I preached some twenty sermons from the pulpit and not once referred to the seventh commandment. I was once challenged by an angry member of the church to do just that: "He is an adulterer," he thundered at me. "Do you believe in the Ten Commandments, or don't you?" Ironically, some three years later, I was appointed as interim minister at another large church whose one-time pastor had also had at least one affair. Again a member of that congregation demanded that I preach on the seventh commandment, and when I did not, accused me of unwillingness to stand up for what is right. After all, he said, if you do not publicly reject behavior that is anathema to our society, are you not tacitly condoning it?

I take these accusations very seriously. And I admit it was a great temptation to proclaim from a position of moral rectitude that the actions of these two pastors were reprehensible, trampling on their wedding vows, demeaning their spouses and their families, and announcing to the world that they were not to be trusted as human beings, not to mention as pastors. In the intervening years I have sometimes wondered whether I had missed my chance to say quite directly that these men's actions were indefensible, that they had shattered the seventh commandment, and had thereby rejected the God who had brought them out of slavery, only to fall back into a new and terrible slavery of their own passions.

However, I continue to reject this public course, and continue to believe that my handling of this part of my task as pastor was the right one. I say this for at least two reasons. First, thundering moralisms lead too often to exclusiveness, self-righteousness, and bigotry. As Jesus so unforgettably said it, looking for the dust mote in the eyes of others blinds us to observing the logs peeking out of our own. To focus on the shortcomings of others can lead us to avoid any shortcomings in ourselves. We humans are prone to chuckling at others, feeling superior to those who have fallen, passing ready judgment on the obvious sinners. We have a hard time learning from the difficulties of others; we would rather sneer, demand retribution, and walk away feeling oh so comfortable in our righteousness. During the recent debacle concerning former President Bill Clinton's inappropriate behavior with the intern Monica Lewinsky, two of his most strident critics, a senior member of the House of Representatives and the man elected to serve as Speaker of that body, both had to admit to adulterous affairs in the glare of public opprobrium. Dust motes so easily blind us to our own logs.

The second reason that I did not employ the direct accusations of the seventh commandment is that I needed to affirm, again and again, that God loves us into God's rule and does not coerce us into it. This is the gospel, found in both Testaments. The phrase of Deuteronomy 7:7, that God chose Israel because God loved them, is matched by the Pauline claim that while we were still weak, Christ died for us (Rom. 5:6). This gospel is true for us, and it is true for the two erring pastors. Unless that gospel is proclaimed clearly and forcefully, we are too often reduced to discussions of behaviors only, what I should or should not be doing. Such discussions are important, but only *after* a clear announcement of the gospel of God has been sounded, that gospel that stands at the base of any and all behaviors.

So, I did not employ the seventh commandment in either of my unusual interim appointments. But it may fairly be asked: what should one do with this commandment? Is it only a dead letter, swept away in a wash of love and good feeling and forgiveness? I do not think so. The seventh commandment still has an important role to play in the right ordering of any society, and the exegesis of the commandment below may provide clues to that ongoing importance. But first we need to offer a brief history of the use of this contentious commandment.

SUBSEQUENT HISTORY OF THE SEVENTH COMMANDMENT

The most famous early commentary on the seventh commandment was provided by the Matthean Jesus who extended the commandment to include even the "lust of the heart," the simple desire to make love to a woman, as a breaking of the commandment (Matt. 5:27-28). We note that the phrase does not include a woman's lustful desires for a man. But Walter Harrelson is surely correct when he says, "[The seventh commandment] will in times to come encourage an application broader than it probably had in view."[1] (See the exegesis below for the rather narrow scope of the biblical formulation.)

This claim was made clear in Luther's Great Catechism when he said that the seventh (Luther's sixth) commandment in fact extended to "every form of unchastity," and that extension included all *thoughts* of unchastity as well. Luther obviously had both men and women in mind when he warned against these behaviors.[2]

Edwin Poteat, moving in a very different direction, speaks for other commentators when he says that the commandment "deals with the towering concept of a man's right to be himself, to be uncorrupted, to be unadulterated, in other words to be free."[3] He goes so far as to state that the verb in question *(na'af)* was not originally concerned with sex.[4]

This is a remarkable claim. It is also not true. The biblical concept, as we shall note, is clearly restricted to sexual impropriety with no hint of an extension into the realm of individual human freedom. Poteat and others have seemingly taken the English word, "adulterate," which means "to make inferior or impure," and have concluded that the seventh commandment has as an extended meaning "do not adulterate," hence do not impose oneself on the freedom of another. Not only does this reading avoid the sexual connotation of the commandment, it moves the meaning into an area of thought more interesting to the modern commentator than to the biblical tradition. The Bible is certainly interested in human freedom, but it is highly suspect to imagine that the seventh commandment has such interest.

In fact, the majority of commentary on this commandment has focused on the sexual implications, most especially broadening those implications to include both men and women. Clovis Chappell, for example, is quick to note that adultery is forbidden as "unfaithfulness on the part of wife or husband," as a sign of "promiscuous marriages," and, like Luther, possesses the extended meaning of "unchastity in thought and deed."[5] R. H. Charles reminds his readers that the "sin of fornication," that is, the sexual act between unmarried consenting adults, was never condemned in the Old Testament as strongly as adultery.[6]

Without question, the seventh commandment has to do with inappropriate sexual intercourse. The exegesis of the commandment will demonstrate this fact.

EXEGESIS OF THE SEVENTH COMMANDMENT

Once again, we must only reckon with one word as we begin our discussion. That Hebrew word is *na'af*. The word is relatively rare, occurring only thirty-four times in all forms in the Hebrew Bible. Its meaning is quite simple to describe. "Analysis of its distribution shows clearly that the term was shaped by the Priestly tradition to denote an offense against marital law."[7] Leviticus 20:10 presents the consequences of transgressing the command: "If a man commits adultery *(na'af)* with the wife of his neighbor, both the adulterer and the adulteress shall be put to death"(NRSV).

This verse, among others, indicates that the marital status of the man is quite irrelevant when considering whether or not adultery has occurred. This is true because a man commits adultery against the woman's *husband*, not against the woman herself, or against his own wife, if he happens to be married. The command is thus indicative of the clear patriarchal culture represented by ancient Israel. A man was granted a great deal more freedom than a woman, and the latter was always seen as the more dangerous and the more responsible party in a sexual relationship. This position is made especially clear in the quite horrific scene described in Numbers 5:11-31.

The tradition enshrined in Numbers 5 says that any man who has "a spirit of jealousy" come over him, that is, if he even slightly suspects that his wife has been unfaithful to him, though he has no proof at all, may bring his wife to the priest, accompanied by the trivial offering of one-tenth of an ephah of barley flour. This tiny offering is described in Leviticus 5:11 as one given by a very poor man who cannot afford the usual sacrificial doves. The woman is then forced to stand before the priest who takes a vessel of holy water and adds a bit of dust from the floor of the temple to the water. He then unbinds her hair, something a woman rarely did in public, and hands to her the small bit of offering grain. Holding the dust-polluted water, the priest demands that the woman, hair unbound in humiliation, repeat a curse against herself. She swears that if she drinks the water, and becomes so sick that "her womb discharges and her uterus drops," she will become "an execration and an oath among the people."

The priest then writes the curse and "washes them" (the letters of the curse?) off into the water. The water, now laced with dust and the words of the curse, is now drunk by the woman. Verses 25-26 imply that the priest also takes a part of the grain offering and burns it on the altar, adding the smoky ashes to the water as well. If upon drinking the water, the woman suffers pains, discharge, and a fallen uterus, she is guilty, but if nothing happens she is declared innocent.

Two things should be noted about this appalling procedure. A man can institute the trial without even a shred of proof that his wife has been unfaithful. And the man pays no consequences even if his accusation is proved false by the trial. "The man shall be free from iniquity," reads verse 31. The cards are so heavily stacked against the woman it is a wonder that any woman so accused could ever survive the trial—and perhaps few finally did.

However, in another place, the husband who makes a false accusation against his new wife does not completely escape punishment. At Deuteronomy 22:13-21, a scenario is described wherein a man, after having intercourse with his bride, decides he just does not like her as well as he thought. So in an attempt to rid himself of her he makes up the charge that she was not a virgin on their wedding night. However, if her parents are able to offer proof that she in fact was a virgin (by showing the bloody bed sheets in the morning after the wedding night—a practice still in evidence in some countries today), the town elders will fine the accusing husband one hundred shekels of silver and give the money to the woman's father. However, if the proof of her virginity is not forthcoming, she shall be hauled out and stoned to death. If the woman is innocent of the false charge, her reward is to remain the wife of the liar who may never divorce her (reward?!). She does not even get any of the fine! If guilty, she is horribly executed. Once again, the woman finds herself generally in an untenable situation with respect to her nearly all-powerful husband.

Proverbs 6:20-35 adds to this patriarchal portrait. Here the one addressed is warned to "keep your father's commandment" (v. 20) which is "a lamp" and "a light" (v. 23). The addressee is warned against the "wife of another" (Hebrew has "the evil woman") who is said to "stalk a man's very life" (v. 26). Two proverbs signal the dangers of this "stalking adulteress."

> Can fire be carried in the bosom
>   without burning one's clothes?
> Or can one walk on hot coals
>   without scorching the feet?
> (vv. 26–27 NRSV)

"No one blames a thief who is hungry for bread" (v. 30),

> But he who commits adultery has no sense;
>   he who does it destroys himself.
> He will get wounds and dishonor,
>   and his disgrace will not be wiped away.
> For jealousy arouses a husband's fury,
>   and he shows no restraint when he takes revenge.
> He will accept no compensation,
>   and refuses a bribe no matter how great.
> (vv. 32–35 NRSV)

The overheated word choice in this poem suggests the deep passions that adultery obviously produced. It is that passion that led to the extreme punishments reserved for adulterers.

In addition to Leviticus 20:10 and its demand for execution both for man and woman caught in adultery, we may add the similar demands of Deuteronomy 22:22. It is clear why the death penalty is called for in these places; the adulteress is not merely a piece of property whose decreased value needs compensation (so Exod. 22:16), but she is rather the wife of a man whose relationship with her has been irredeemably profaned and his reputation sullied.

The prophets of Israel also borrowed this language for adultery and used it to describe the painful relationship that too often existed between God and God's people. The eighth-century B.C.E. Hosea found in the language of adultery the very center of his understanding of his prophetic vocation. He married the woman Gomer, who was first a prostitute and later an adulteress. In fact, for Hosea the two words become nearly synonymous. Hosea's marriage to Gomer is a mirror for him of the strained connection between YHWH and Israel, Israel being the wanton adulteress and YHWH the wounded but faithful husband. Later, the sixth-century B.C.E. Ezekiel rang obscene changes on the theme in two lengthy allegories of the God-Israel relationship. In chapter 16, Israel is said to be a bastard child, abandoned to die, but saved by YHWH. However, the pampered and protected child grew up to become a prostitute, selling herself to every passerby. As in Hosea, the words prostitute and adulteress become synonymous for Ezekiel as Israel refuses even to be paid for her sexual favors and becomes thereby an "adulteress wife, who receives strangers instead of her husband" (Ezek. 16:32). And in chapter 23, the allegory of Oholah and Oholibah, northern Israel and southern Judah in thin disguise, are also described as wanton lovers, prostitutes and adulteresses.

Such charged sexual language, blatant and abrupt in its accusations, while providing unforgettable portraits of prophetic power, have at the same time done grave damage to the images of women offered by the Bible's pages.[8] Pornography is no less pornographic by existing in the Bible! Preachers should be very careful if and when they use this sort of imagery in sermons; they could, quite unintentionally but no less surely, reinforce a female stereotype of looseness or wantonness. It just may be that the imagery, as forceful and memorable as it is, needs not to be used in the pulpits of the twenty-first century, given the widespread confusions in the culture concerning issues of gender and sex.

Without doubt, the most famous case of the application of the patriarchal laws occurs in the New Testament story of the birth of Jesus. Mary, a woman betrothed to Joseph, becomes pregnant and offers the absurd excuse that she is with child by the Holy Spirit of God. In law, Joseph, publicly humiliated by his fiancée's obvious infidelity, decides to "dismiss her quietly," even though he has every right to accuse her openly and have her stoned to death (so Leviticus and Deuteronomy). An angel warns him that the story of the Holy Spirit's involvement is true.

Two other very famous stories of the results of adultery and sexual misconduct are found in the accounts of the life of King David. In 2 Samuel 11 we find the astonishing tale of David and Bathsheba. The king, already possessed of many wives (seven are named for us to this point in the story) is smitten by the bathing Bathsheba and begins an adulterous affair with her. It is adulterous because she is married to one of David's mercenary generals, Uriah the Hittite. Within the confines of this one chapter, it could be said that David breaks fully half of the Ten Commandments: he has killed, he has committed adultery, he has coveted, he has lied against his neighbor, and he has stolen the woman away from her husband. The results are disastrous in the extreme. One after another, David's children assault one another (Amnon rapes Tamar), kill one another (Absalom kills Amnon), and finally depose their own father from his kingship (Absalom throws David out of Jerusalem). No more graphic tale of the inevitable horrors of adultery could be imagined.

The second story is wrapped up in the one just described. In 2 Samuel 13, Amnon rapes his half-sister, Tamar. Strictly speaking, this assault is not adultery since Tamar is not married or betrothed. The powerful Tamar, even while she is being assaulted, begs the lusty Amnon to "speak to the king who will not withhold me from you." Marriage would be possible, but rape will lead to disaster for both of them. And so it does. The results of the rape are ignominious solitude for Tamar (she simply disappears from the story) and death for Amnon, murdered by the enraged and protective Absalom. In fact, the latter acts just like an aggrieved husband, exacting his revenge on the merciless would-be adulterer. [9]

The passionate power of the ritual accounts of Numbers and Deuteronomy, and the riveting tales of 2 Samuel 11 and 13 give evidence of the surging emotions generated by sexuality deemed inappropriate by Israelite law and custom. Our exegesis of the seventh commandment suggests the following conclusions.

1

No clearer indication of the second-class citizenship of women in ancient Israel may be found than in an examination of the laws and customs surrounding adultery. The double standard for women is clear and continuous throughout. Only a few glimmers toward equality may be glimpsed, such as Deuteronomy's demand that the lying husband be forced to pay something monetarily for his lies. Such tiny flashes must have occurred now and then, as women began to call for more of their rights as full partners in marriages and in community. In our own time, we need to move ever closer to a full equality between the sexes, something basically unknown in the culture that nurtured our Bible.

2

Sex is dangerous, emotional, and given over to excesses, both in its practices and in its punishments. Deep mystery marks the ways of sexuality. In the section of the Proverbs known as the "Sayings of Agur," we read:

> Three things are too wonderful for me;
>   four I do not understand:
> the way of an eagle in the sky,
>   the way of a snake on a rock,
> the way of a ship on the high seas,
>   and the way of a man with a girl.
>   (30:18-19 NRSV)

These lovely metaphors about the mysteries of sexuality are, however, followed by the fateful warning about the frightful dangers of the *wrong* woman. "This is the way of the adulteress: she eats, and wipes her mouth, and says, 'I have done no wrong.'" This near pornographic verse reminds the reader of the dangers of sexuality just after she or he has been warmed by the wonders of sexuality. So it is in the Hebrew Bible. Sex is God's good gift, but sex is also fraught with traps and pitfalls. The result of falling in could be death.

SERMONIC NOTES

1

A sermon on the seventh commandment could take as its subject the wonders and dangers of God's gift of human sexuality. The church has often been loath to discuss openly this very basic experience of our humanity. Too often the church has been merely against sex, seeing it either as an impediment to true spirituality or as a major demon on the road to excess and degradation. To see sexual activity as God's great gift to us is not to tempt the unwary to lewd behavior; it is to affirm a beautiful and wondrous fact of our lives together.

At the same time, to speak against the wrongful use of sex, to warn against the dangers of sex practiced with the spouse of another, and against one's own spouse, is not to play the prude in a permissive society. As I said above, in my two interim pastorates, where sexual misconduct was on the minds of all my listeners, I did not address the question of sexuality directly, feeling that a more basic presentation of the gospel was needed in those situations. Still a discussion of the power of the seventh commandment, and the dangers to the self and the community of its transgression, is important in a culture all too prone to dismiss such prohibitions out of hand.

2

A sermon on the seventh commandment could discuss the implications of the inequality of men and women. After discussing the details of the cultural context of the commandment, the preacher could move toward the issue of gender inequality. The negative impact on women of the amazing accounts of Numbers 5 and Deuteronomy 22 could be highlighted, and the congregation urged to move beyond such stereotyping. Though these cases are extreme, and partake of a good deal of magical belief to make their points, what are the many ways in which women are stereotyped and stripped of equality in our own time? A sermon with this subject, especially out of the mouth of a male preacher, could have a powerful effect on women and men alike.

3

A more specific focus on the community impact of the transgression of the seventh commandment could be important. In what specific ways is the community thrown into chaos and turmoil when adultery is discovered? Divorce often ensues, children are profoundly affected, grandparents are left in confusion, communities of churches, clubs, neighborhoods are forced to alter their perceptions of each person in the family. And each individual influenced by the adulterous behavior must reorient themselves to the changed situation. Some will be angry, some sad, some shattered, some on the surface indifferent; all will never be the same. Adultery has enormous consequences, some predictable, many unpredictable. The fabric of a community is forever torn, and the process of reweaving is sometimes slow, sometimes impossible. Those who would say that what goes on in our bedrooms is nobody's business are naïve fools. Sex with another's partner unleashes forces that threaten to swallow the world, or at the very least to chew our part of it into a messy pulp. These realities need to be spoken from our pulpits, spoken in love to be sure, but spoken nonetheless.

CHAPTER EIGHT

The Eighth Commandment

You must not steal.

For the third consecutive commandment we are faced with two Hebrew words only: this time, *Lo' tignob*. As in the previous two commandments against killing and adultery, this eighth commandment sounds a very general proscription against an all-too-familiar human behavior. Theft is something as old as the existence of the word "mine." The minute one person determined and proclaimed that she had something of her own, another person sought to take it from her. The very oldest law codes we possess, well summarized and codified in the famous Code of Hammurabi (eighteenth and seventeenth centuries B.C.E.), deal with various kinds of theft at length, offering quite gruesome punishments for certain sorts of thievery. For example, the theft of children requires the death penalty, as does theft of temple or royal items. In fact, in other cases of the most serious thefts, death was the punishment as well, while embezzlement of seed required the cutting off of the hands. However, in later editions of the Code, an assessment of fines seemed to replace some of the earlier demands for physical restitution.

In Assyrian law (perhaps as old as the fifteenth century B.C.E.), theft by a wife was punishable by death, while other penalties for thievery were ear and nose mutilation, flogging with rods, and forced labor. However, as in the later versions of Hammurabi's Code, Assyrian laws (eighth to seventh centuries) mention only fines in cash or goods as punishment.

The laws of the Hittites (perhaps as early as the thirteenth century B.C.E.) mention only fines for various acts of theft with the single exception of the theft of a bronze lance from the palace gate! That theft alone is punishable by death.[1]

This cursory summation of the vast corpus of ancient Middle Eastern law indicates the tremendous interest in the appropriate regulation of stealing in all cultures. Theft was quite obviously a problem everywhere. When comparing these ancient codes with the comments on theft in the Hebrew Bible, perhaps the following generalization may be made: "The essential difference between these laws and the Old Testament is that the punishments for crimes of theft in extrabiblical laws are much more rigorous. In the early period especially, punishment by death and mutilation was not rare in the ancient Near East, even for stealing possessions."[2] Of course, this general difference may be the result of the fact that the laws of the Hebrew Bible are comparatively late in time and may have had the benefit of the lengthy struggle that earlier cultures had to arrive at the most appropriate ways to deal with the problem of theft.

This great problem has hardly disappeared in our own day. Property crime occurs in the United States every ten seconds on average! The highly successful consumer culture that we have created generates a huge demand for goods; indeed our capitalist system is driven by this demand. If we do not go and buy, the system falters. Persons are too often evaluated on the basis of their possessions, the right car, the right neighborhood, the diversified portfolio, the correct vacation, the easy retirement, even the classiest funeral! Such desirable items feed the natural human concern for pleasure and comfort and envy. We *all* must have these things! But of course we cannot *all* have them. Those who cannot buy them, sometimes resort to stealing them, if not the objects themselves, at least the money with which to buy them. If the mantra of our consumer culture is, "The one with the most toys wins," the desire for "toys" is well-nigh insatiable.

In the face of the gale-force of wants, how can a two-word commandment make any real difference? "You must not steal," it says, but if my worth, my image, and my very life are supposed to be determined by what I have, rather than by what I am, no little command against stealing will stop the raging of my lusts for things. It is hardly enough, as so many have found, to shout, "Just say No" in the face of the lure of drugs; neither will any simple repetition of "Don't steal" stanch the river of my desire.

This certain fact provides a possible clue to the continued value of the eighth commandment. Such a commandment is only necessary in a society where a few have a lot and many have only a little. In such a situation the command against stealing could be seen as a ploy by the rich to keep what they have from the poor who have nothing, but who are told at the same time that what the rich have are the best things in all the world to have. As Walter Eichrodt says, "This commandment does far more than protect property. It warns against taking advantage of a brother (or sister) in need. It stands against all exploitation of the weak, and is a guide for all social and economic action and restraint." [3] If society more resembled the earliest Christian community described in the Acts of the Apostles 4:32-37, both the desire for vast wealth and the desire to steal from those who have it would be seriously curtailed. The commandment against stealing is more than a guarantee of the inviolability of private property; it is an announcement that all societies need a basic reordering where the conditions for theft are not so evident. Such a reordering was needed in ancient Babylon and Assyria and Israel, and surely is needed in the modern United States.

THE SUBSEQUENT HISTORY OF THE EIGHTH COMMANDMENT

The expansion in meaning of the eighth commandment suggested in my introduction above was anticipated by Martin Luther in his Great Catechism. His discussion begins with the obvious thieves, those who are actually caught taking things not their own, but quickly moves to those whom Luther calls "gentlemen swindlers" and "big operators." [4] These more dangerous "thieves" (though they are rarely so branded) are the wealthy few who own too much and care too little, who sit atop the economic ladder at the expense of the many poor. Luther very easily hears in the eighth commandment a sharp attack on economic *and* social injustice. [5] His keen insights are not limited by the notion that this commandment is only about private property rights.

He is able to move in this direction because he is so thoroughly steeped in the social justice concerns of the Hebrew Bible, living as he did in a time when the vast gulf between rich and poor was becoming ever more obvious and ever more dangerous. We noted earlier the huge peasant revolt during his lifetime, engendered at least in part by the grinding poverty of the many in the face of the unimaginable luxuries of the few. And even though he reacted with a cruel horror to the chaos the revolt unleashed, he could not have failed to notice the conditions that led to that revolt. Certainly his commentary on this commandment suggests clearly that he was aware of those terrible conditions.

A rather more conservative response was offered by R. H. Charles in 1923 England. After a brief series of statements announcing the horrors of stealing, Charles turns quickly toward the "excesses of the Trade Unions," those groups who demanded a larger share of the economic pie. For Charles, the eighth commandment does indeed ensure the rights of private property and also commends owners of that property to be good stewards of that which is bestowed on them by a gracious God.[6] One could hardly find a better example of the influence of one's social position on the reading of the biblical text. Charles, a privileged and comfortable English cleric and academic, would have a great deal to lose if the eighth commandment had the economic implications within it that Luther saw. Of course, my own readings are also affected enormously by my social location as an equally privileged and comfortable academic! I can only hope that I see clearly that privilege and comfort, and never assume that my readings are the only, even the best, possible ones.

Fifteen years later in 1938, the Methodist preacher Clovis Chappell, in many essentials, agreed with Luther's reading but expanded the commandment's meaning to include taking "by stealth or force that which rightly belongs to another… whether the values stolen were tangible or intangible."[7] Such things could include physical objects, of course, but reputations could just as easily be stolen. Chappell says that verbal attacks with the attempt to destroy character are a violation of the eighth commandment because they constitute such thefts of reputation. And he goes one step further, claiming that "withholding what we ought to give" also constitutes stealing. This latter claim runs the risk we have seen before, namely widening a commandment's scope so far as to make it finally meaningless. After all, the determination of "what we ought to give" is so fraught with complexity and disagreement that in certain eyes practically *anything* I do not freely give to someone else could constitute theft.

Fifteen years still later, Edwin Poteat says that the eighth commandment enshrines the constant struggle of society's restraint "on corporate or individual self-aggrandizement."[8] This need for restraint is "the heart of the political struggle." That struggle for Poteat in 1953 is the struggle against communism as made manifest in the Soviet Union and its Marxist-Leninist economic system, most especially its collective ideas of the means of production. And, of course, the fact that the Soviet system was publicly atheistic made this struggle far more than an intellectual one for mid-century Christians. In the light of that struggle, economic and deeply emotional, Poteat claims that "thou shalt not steal suggests that man has not abdicated his moral right to own things that make for freedom and peace."[9] Thus, Poteat sees the need for restraint in our rampant capitalistic consumerism, but he also wants to say clearly that private property is no bad thing, if it is used in the service of "freedom and peace." Once again, the social location of a commentator plays a huge role in the reading of a biblical text.

This brief history suggests three possible meanings for the eighth commandment.

1. It could offer a sharp prophetic rejoinder against inequitable distributions of wealth, creating the context where theft is common (Luther among others).

2. It could enshrine the importance of the concept of private property, both tangible and intangible (Charles and Chappell with different emphases).

3. Yet, to the contrary, it could also demand a sharp restraint on social and personal self-aggrandizement (Poteat).

A commandment that has been used to defend private property *and* inveigh against the inequalities of wealth due to the excess of private property needs a careful exegesis with hope of discovering clues toward which of these disparate meanings seems the more likely.

EXEGESIS OF THE EIGHTH COMMANDMENT

The semantic field of the Hebrew verb, *ganab*, extends from "removing (secretly) to cheating."[10] The objects of the verb "to steal" are in general three.

1

The most basic one is possessions. In small agriculturally and pastorally constituted communities, theft of animals must have been a serious problem. Hence, the very general legal maxim of Exodus 22:1 (Hebrew, English, 22:2): "If a thief is found breaking in (at night), and is beaten to death, there is no blood-guilt." This means that a nighttime burglar who is killed by the victim receives what he deserved; the victim is guilty of nothing in defending his/her property. But, to the contrary, if the thief attempts to steal in the daytime, and is killed by the property owner, that owner *does* incur blood-guilt. So, unlike the harsher laws of theft found in Hammurabi's Code, the Hebrew Bible makes a distinction between the uncertainties and dangers of nighttime intrusions and the daytime crime where help could be more readily expected before killing was needed for self-defense.

Just prior to this general proscription of Exodus 22:1, we read, "When someone steals an ox or a sheep, and slaughters it or sells it, the thief shall pay five oxen for an ox and four sheep for a sheep" (NRSV), the former being obviously more valuable than the latter. Death is here not a punishment for theft, but restitution. And "when the animal, ox, donkey or sheep, is found alive in the thief's hand, the thief pays (only) double" (22:3 Heb., 22:4 Eng.). Again, the laws move away from physical punishment toward restitution. Later in this same chapter (Exod. 22:6-8 Heb., 7-9 Eng.) the law is that when money or property are brought to a house for safe-keeping, and the things are stolen, the apprehended thief shall "pay double." But if the thief is not caught, then the owner of the house where the money or property was brought for safe-keeping "is brought before God" (apparently in some sort of ritual trial) to see whether the owner himself stole the money or property entrusted to him. Verse 8 (9 Eng.) lays down the general rule that "any case of disputed ownership," whether ox, donkey, sheep, clothing, or any other lost item, "shall come before God" for ritual adjudication. The loser of the trial shall pay double to the winner.

Perhaps the most famous story of theft in the Hebrew Bible is found in Joshua 7. The Israelites, under the leadership of Joshua, have made a miraculous crossing of the Jordan and have entered the land of promise. Immediately we are told that Achan, one of the people of Israel, has taken certain valuable objects from their conquered enemies, objects that God had commanded to be destroyed. The army's subsequent attack on the sparsely defended city of Ai is surprisingly repulsed, and the army flees in retreat. General Joshua is shocked and humiliated, crying out to YHWH for explanation for the defeat. YHWH tells him that there is a thief among them, and as long as that thief is alive, and is hoarding his stolen goods, Israel is doomed. By careful selection Achan is found out, admits his theft, and is stoned and burned—he, his family, and all his possessions, both stolen and rightfully his.

Though death is the result of Achan's theft, it is certainly no ordinary theft. This one theft curses the entire community, and unless the perpetrator is expunged the community cannot survive. The fact that this one unique example of theft leading to death is so memorable that this lengthy tale remains in our text suggests yet again that capital punishment for stealing was extremely rare in Israel.

The most famous theft story in the New Testament is surely John's account of Judas Iscariot (John 12:4-6). Mary, the sister of Lazarus, takes a large amount of very expensive perfume, pours it on Jesus' feet, and wipes it lovingly with her unbound hair. Judas, smelling the pungent fragrance, regrets the enormous waste that Mary's gift represents. The three hundred denarii (nearly a year's wage for a laborer) could have been sold and the proceeds distributed among the poor, Judas says. However, in one of John's inside observations, he tells the reader that nasty Judas, the soon-to-be betrayer of Jesus, did not in fact have the poor in mind when he said this. He is a thief, says John, and he regrets the loss of money the perfume would have fetched, since it will reduce the common purse from which he has been regularly stealing. This ugly story about the most maligned figure in the Gospel story emphasizes the great opprobrium that theft engendered in the ancient world.

2

The second object of the verb "to steal" is people. It has been suggested that the most basic meaning of the eighth commandment is in fact a law against kidnap. Given the several objects of the verb, that supposition is hardly likely, or is at least finally unprovable. Yet, Exodus 21:16 states, "Anyone who steals a person (kidnaps), whether that person has been sold or is still held by the thief, shall be executed." This very general law, suggesting nothing of nationality or status as slave or free, is made more restrictive in Deuteronomy 24:7. "If anyone is found stealing another Israelite, then enslaving or selling him, that thief shall die." It is usually assumed that the implication of the Exodus passage is the same as that of the more restrictive Deuteronomy verse. However, the Exodus verse is universally thought to be older than the Deuteronomy, and it is at least conceivable that the early law of emergent Israel could have tended toward a rejection of *any* stealing, or any buying and selling, of *any* person. Hence, this could be a calling into question of the practice of slavery itself. But given what we know about the common slave practices of the ancient Near East, that possibility may be little more than romantic wishful thinking.

Again, there is a famous narrative illustration of kidnap. Joseph has been "put away" by his brothers when they (or the Midianites; the text is ambiguous) sell him to Ishmaelite traders bound for Egypt (Gen. 37:28). When Joseph recounts this scene to his fellow prisoners in Egypt, pharaoh's chief baker and cupbearer, he says that he "was stolen out of the land of the Hebrews" (Gen. 40:15 NRSV). His use of the verb indicates the seriousness of the charge. He has been kidnapped with the clear intent that he die, either on the arduous journey to Egypt or after his arrival and enslavement there. By the laws of Exodus and Deuteronomy, his brothers are fully worthy of death. The theft of a person, kidnap, is not taken lightly in Israel. That seriousness is matched in our own day, where kidnappings are seen as especially heinous crimes in special instances worthy of death.

3

The third object of the verb "to steal" comprises various metaphorical meanings. For example, in Genesis 31:20, 26, 27, the aggrieved Laban, father-in-law of the wily Jacob, accuses the trickster three times of "stealing his heart" (i.e., "deceiving him"). Because the word "heart" in Hebrew primarily refers to the place of will and intelligence, for Laban to say that Jacob has stolen his heart (mind) is quite literally true. He has been tricked out of wealth, especially livestock, daughters, and grandchildren; they have been stolen from him. A slightly different nuance is found in 2 Samuel 15:6. David's ambitious son, Absalom, schemes to take the throne of his aging and indolent father by "kissing" supplicants at the palace gate, thus "stealing the hearts of the people of Israel." Modern politicians have nothing on the unctuous Absalom! In this context there may indeed by an element of deception in the use, in the manner of Laban's understanding, but here the emphasis seems to be on the wooing away by hard work and persistence rather than on outright trickery. Nevertheless, the result is the same: hearts are stolen.

In later passages like Hosea 4:2 and Jeremiah 7:9 the mention of "stealing" among a general list of evil acts sounds like a reference to the Decalogue in some early form. "Stealing" in these contexts is simply a sign of general Israelite depravity concerning which YHWH is furious. It is interesting to note that only in one place in these later texts does one find a discussion of punishment for theft. And that discussion is only used as an example of the larger issue of the punishments for adulterers (see my discussion in the previous chapter).

> Thieves are not despised who steal only
>   to satisfy their appetite when hungry.
> Yet if they are caught, they will pay sevenfold;
>   (compare Deut. and Exod. above)
> they will forfeit all the goods of their house.
> (Prov. 6:30-31 NRSV)

Even in one of the greatest chapters in Scripture addressing the issues of moral behavior, Job 31, theft is not directly mentioned. This general indifference to theft in Israel's later literature may suggest that even restitution to victims became unimportant to Israel.[11] However, we should be very hesitant to make such sweeping generalizations with so little direct evidence. As we have said, theft was and is a problem in any culture that possesses even a modicum of commercial activity. How to deal with it, how to curb it and punish it, are issues that will always be with us.

SERMONIC NOTES

1

A sermon on the eighth commandment may address the enormous impact of theft on a community. Anyone who has suffered theft of property goes through a series of emotions. I have been burglarized two times in my life. The first was when my son was three years old. The young thieves broke into our house, and, among other things, they smashed his piggy bank and stole all his collected pennies and nickels. My son is twenty-seven years old, and he still vividly recalls the day when his bank was robbed. There is a deep violation we feel when we suffer theft. And there is fear. We are finally not completely safe in our own homes. Thieves with the will and the time and the tools can enter any place, no matter how protected, and steal our things. The second theft I suffered was from an apartment I was renting. The thieves smashed in my front door and took nearly everything not nailed down: TV, radio, stereo, all compact discs (some 150), lamps, toaster, and so forth. I was devastated! I was mad! I was afraid! I was violated! I was told that in over 95 percent of these cases of theft, the stolen objects are never recovered (amazingly, I got mine back, less the CDs).

What effects does theft have on individuals in community? The emotions I felt, and still feel, though my last theft experience was over ten years ago, are deep and lasting. I am a bit less trusting, a bit more suspicious, a bit more angry, a bit more likely to be cynical rather than hopeful, a bit more fearful, especially at night. These feelings certainly affect my standing in my community, how I view laws against theft, how I evaluate the authorities' willingness and ability to make my world safer. What resources does the Christian faith bring to bear on these profound and important emotions? Many members of all congregations will have suffered theft. What can we say to their emotions? What does the gospel say to this kind of physical theft? What positive steps can a congregation take to help communities in danger?

2

Following Luther's lead, the eighth commandment can focus the congregation's attention on the larger issue of the inequitable distribution of wealth in a society that prizes wealth nearly beyond all things. Most Americans can tell you who the world's richest person is (currently Bill Gates), but 75 percent of them cannot list the four Gospels of the New Testament, and even fewer could tell you that the single most frequently mentioned subject in those Gospels is in fact the dangers of wealth! By every measure we have, the gap between rich and poor in our increasingly interconnected world is growing larger by the year. In the Spring of 2001 I made a ten-day trip to El Salvador, a tiny country the size of Delaware, population six million. After a long and devastating civil war, financed in large part by the United States, and after two huge earthquakes in 2001, 50 percent of Salvadorans have no stable shelter and no jobs. During the civil war (1979–1991), the United States gave to the government of the country approximately $1,000,000 per day to fight the war. The total amount was at least $3,000,000,000. After the earthquakes, our United States government pledged $110,000,000 in aid, half of which are loans to be repaid, and half of which we took from the aid budget for Haiti, the poorest country in the Western Hemisphere.

When I returned to the United States, I flew in a plane for two and a half hours to arrive in Houston, Texas. In that one airport, there were concentrated more wealth, more goods and services, than probably existed in all of El Salvador. Surely such gross inequities demand a response. "You must not steal" takes on a powerful sound when set against the vast discrepancies I saw after those two and a half hours.

3

I am struck by the possible importance of the expanded meaning of the eighth commandment that is concerned with the theft of character, that is the cynical assault on others so endemic in our society. I find it helpful to think about this action as a real kind of theft. The amazing popularity of a whole generation of TV shows—the several "Survivor" series, the newest *Weakest Link*, the chaotic talk shows like Jerry Springer and Montel Williams among a host of others—all bear witness that our culture enjoys watching real people triumph, but more often fall into terrible behaviors characterized by excess, envy, and physical fury. In watching these programs we demean ourselves, reducing our brothers and sisters, and thus ourselves, to a base form of humanity, ruled by greed, power, and victory at all costs. Also, when *People* magazine is the most read periodical in the United States, and when salacious journalism in the *Enquirer* or *Globe* appears to be little different at times from the regular daily paper, our thirst for lewd tidbits about the personal lives of the rich and famous, or the once-rich and once-famous, suggest that our theft of basic humanity breaks the eighth commandment. The theft of a person's reputation is surely as terrible as the theft of that person's car. And the theft of a community's sense of itself, its hope in its basic goodness, is surely as terrible as the theft of money. Howard Stern's assaults on common morality, and Gordon Liddy's and Rush Limbaugh's intemperate attacks on people who do not share their particular political ideas, debase all of us to the level of school yard name-calling.

And such theft of reputation is not found only in the popular media and in the political arena. In the world of religion, theft like this occurs on a regular basis. The pastor of a large church in San Antonio, Texas, with a huge TV presence sends literally millions of Christians weekly (Methodists, Roman Catholics, Presbyterians, Pentecostals, et al.) to the hell he quite literally believes in, simply because they do not hew to the theological and/or political line that he espouses. Such hate-filled attacks, often uttered under the false guise of the love of God, also warn us against theft of reputation, the stealing of another human's real self.

And how many of our own religious expositions inadvertently steal the reputations of others? When we inveigh against the Jews of the Bible, "who killed Jesus," what anti-Semitism do we harbor in ourselves and kindle in our hearers? When we label someone a "liberal" (usually with the adjective "fuzzy-headed") or a "conservative" (usually with the adjective "neanderthal"), do we not steal something from them, their rich human complexity and their complex human potentialities? When viewed in this light, the eighth commandment becomes nothing less than a call to a more loving humanity, a more caring inclusiveness. Such a sermon on the eighth commandment needs hearing from our twenty-first-century pulpits.

CHAPTER NINE

The Ninth Commandment

You must not answer against your neighbor a lying witness.
(Exod. 20:16)

You must not answer against your neighbor an empty witness.
(Deut. 5:20)

INTRODUCTION

The ninth commandment presents us with two forms, very close in formulation but with one interesting difference. The proscription against "false" witness, as the traditional translation reads, is in fact modified by two important words. The Exodus formulation warns against a "lying" witness, a word that bears the basic connotation of "untruth." The Deuteronomy version describes an "empty" witness, reminiscent of the warning of the third commandment against lifting up YHWH's name for "emptiness" or "nothingness." (See the discussion of the word in chapter three). Though a "lying" witness and an "empty" witness may amount to nearly the same thing in a court of law, there are subtle distinctions between the two words that we will address in the exegesis.

The obvious setting for the wording of the ninth commandment is a law court. The words "answer" and "neighbor" and "witness" suggest a formalized setting of the examination of evidence. Of course, we twenty-first century people should not anachronize this setting so much as to miss the many possible locations in which such legal examinations might have taken place in ancient Israel. Law courts then might appear rather informal to us. For example, in the fourth chapter of the book of Ruth, Boaz, who has just spent a romantic evening on the threshing floor with the Moabite widow, Ruth, stands at the "gate of the city" in order to begin a legal proceeding wherein he hopes to gain the legal right to marry the widow. It appears in this account that Boaz himself calls the "court" together, choosing "ten men of the elders of the city (Bethlehem)" to serve as jury, and calling the rival "next-of-kin" to the domestic trial (Ruth 4:1-2). Boaz, after asking the unnamed next-of-kin and the gathered jury to sit down, offers a stylized speech, focusing deceptively on land acquisitions in connection with Ruth's property ownership. We hardly imagine that land purchase was uppermost on Boaz's mind while dallying with Ruth on the threshing floor!

Nevertheless, he speaks only of land and asks the next-of-kin, who has by law prior rights to the property of Ruth (see Deut. 25:5–10), to purchase that property, since it is his for the buying. However, says Boaz, if the next-of-kin does not wish to exercise his rights, then Boaz will be glad to do so, since he is next in line for the property of Ruth. The next-of-kin first welcomes the chance to get some more property. But Boaz then tells him that with the property comes Ruth, the Moabite, a childless widow whose future children would inherit the property of Ruth's dead husband, leaving the next-of-kin with all the financial responsibility and no financial gain. The next-of-kin wants no part of such a possible dead-end bargain and hands the right of purchase to Boaz. Boaz is only too glad to gain this right, since he wishes to marry the marvelous Ruth, a "woman of worth" (3:11), fully equal to the prominent Boaz, who was earlier named "a man of worth" (2:1), using the identical phrase in Hebrew.

We learn from this rich account that the lower court of Israel was regularly the gate of the city, that place through which many workers and traders passed. As the place of entrance and exit, it, along with the wells of the community, naturally became gathering places where people swapped stories, transacted business, and on occasion held legal proceedings. In another example, Absalom, David's ambitious and rebellious son, "stole the hearts of the people of Israel" from his father by standing each morning "beside the road into the gate," and making legal judgments for those who had come to receive justice from the king (2 Sam. 15:2). And the prophet Amos, while castigating the social evils of the people of Israel, singled out the gate, the hopeful place of justice, as a place where "the needy" are instead "pushed aside" (Amos 5:12). To the contrary, Amos demands in the name of YHWH that Israel "Hate evil and love good, and establish justice in the gate" (5:15). Amos makes plain what the ninth commandment demands: truth-telling in the court, wherever such courts may be held. If one cannot get truth and justice in the court, then truth and justice are unavailable in any place where laws attempt to regulate the behaviors of members of a community. Lack of justice in court leads to a lack of justice in the wider community.

How well our modern world knows this truth! We depend on our court system to discover truth amid the complexities that life in community present to us. When O. J. Simpson was acquitted of the murder of his wife and her friend, many thought that justice had been purchased by a wealthy and famous athlete; the decision was deeply tainted for many. When the recent presidential election (2000) was too close to call in the state of Florida, we expected our judicial system to rule definitively on the confusion. The five to four ruling of the United States Supreme Court to stop all post-election ballot counting, and thus to give the victory to George Bush, clearly had the final force of law, although it appeared to many that the politics of some of the justices had been as significant in the decision as the law. However, we United States citizens expected our judiciary to sort out the mess, and when they did just that, to the satisfaction of some and the anger of others, no one took up arms or declared war to reverse the decision. In a community ultimately ruled by law, the courts have ultimate authority.

This notion of the rule of law in the Western world is simply taken for granted now. Since the fledgling attempt to curb the power of wealth and status at Runnymede, England in 1215 C.E. in the signing of the Magna Carta, our part of the world has moved inexorably, if at times fitfully, toward the rule of law. But, this ninth commandment enshrines within its few words one of the bedrock ideas of our civilization, though it predates Magna Carta by at least fifteen hundred years.

THE SUBSEQUENT HISTORY OF THE NINTH COMMANDMENT

It is fair to say that the history of the explications and use of the ninth commandment are the least contentious of all the Ten Commandments. Nearly every commentator reads the commandment as a warning against lying in court and comments at length on the great dangers to the community when such lying occurs. In some instances the meaning of the commandment is extended to include other sorts of lying. For example, Luther in the Large Catechism contends that this commandment includes most especially "false preachers and heretics."[1] The twentieth century Methodist, Clovis Chappell, claims that the commandment warns all of us to "control our tongues," which leads him to a discussion of the horrors of slander and gossip, quite often the bane of churches.[2]

But the fact that "bearing false witness" (as the KJV has it) has become a well-known phrase in our secular vocabulary, is eloquent proof that the ninth commandment has through the centuries borne the primary force of lying in legal contexts. The Bible itself bears this out. Several texts make plain the great importance the ancient community placed on truth-telling in courts. In the midst of the Holiness Code in Exodus, generally believed to be among the earliest of the codes found in the Hebrew Bible, chapter 23:1-3 addresses some details concerning lying witnesses.

> You must not carry an empty report. You must not join hands with the wicked to become a violent witness. You must not follow after the many for evil; when you witness in a lawsuit, you must not side with the many to act sinfully. You must not favor the poor in a lawsuit.

This passage is replete with important ideas concerning the dangers of lying and false witnesses.

1

One example of a breaking of the ninth commandment is to "carry an empty report." The NRSV translates this: "You shall not spread a false report." This has enormous consequences for the community. A report of behaviors and/or words, repeated without factual foundation, can serve as a death warrant for the innocent. And when such reports are repeated in court, that death can become quite real. In 1 Kings 21, we find the most memorable instance of the use of an "empty report" to destroy an innocent man. We have discussed this scene at length above in connection with the eighth commandment, but briefly: Ahab's demand for Naboth's vineyard leads his wife Jezebel to pay two witnesses to bring a false report about Naboth's behavior to the community, which is gathered at a celebration in honor of that same Naboth. The lying report of the two witnesses leads to Naboth's death by stoning and the theft of his vineyard by the king.

2

"Joining hands with wicked people" to become thereby a "violent witness" (NRSV "malicious witness") is another way to break the ninth commandment. If one becomes part of a plot to defame a person, offering malicious and violent witness designed to destroy the innocent, the commandment is shattered. By this account, Ahab, Jezebel, and the two lying witnesses against Naboth have clearly broken the ninth commandment and have pushed their community over the precipice of deep-seated injustice.

3

You must not follow the majority opinion just because it is a majority. The simple phrase "majority rules" can be deadly. In the American South, it was certainly the case that the majority of the white population believed that segregation was the right thing to do. Looking back on such a belief some fifty years later, a new majority would just as surely say that segregation was a great wrong. In the movie and play, *Twelve Angry Men*, a jury is sequestered to decide the fate of a man believed to be guilty by eleven of the jurors. Only one has the slightest doubt. Through the course of the gripping drama, one by one the jurors change their minds as their prejudice and bigotry are unmasked by the one dogged juror who is unwilling to allow the majority to rule merely because it is a majority. In the end, the easy "majority rules" concept is shown to be dangerously false. Strength may be found in numbers, but truth does not necessarily reside there.

4

"Neither should you favor the poor in a lawsuit." Being poor gives a person no special rights before the court of law. This is an

important and complex idea in any community. A community of
law often speaks of "equal justice" for all of its citizens, yet all in
the community know that certain members, because of wealth or
status, have a better chance at full justice than do those who have
little wealth and no status. Hence, some communities have
attempted to right the wrongs of this systemic injustice by providing employment "set-asides" for certain disempowered groups in
order that more members of the community may have access to
more goods and services in that community. This may indeed be a
helpful tactic to "even the playing field," however controversial it
may be.

However, in a court of law, says Exodus 23:3, there can be no
partiality toward the poor, just as surely as there can be none for
the rich. Societal injustice should not be corrected in the judgments of courts; we cannot wait for our courts, in the process of
adjudicating our laws, to correct injustices on their own. If in the
South of the 1940s and 50s, we expected the courts to change
unjust laws, we would have been forever disappointed. The people of the South, both black and white, had to express publicly
their dissatisfaction with the written laws before change was possible. No court then, or now, should be expected to right injustice
by ruling in favor of a defendant strictly on the basis of his or her
skin color or economic status. The fact that in rare instances, courts
may do precisely that is no sign that that is the business of such
decisions. In a community ruled by law, Exodus 23:1-3 is surely
right; strict impartiality and strict truth-telling in court are the
hallmarks of a viable society.

Other biblical texts are important as commentary on the ninth
commandment. In discussing the details of how a witness's truth-
telling is to be evaluated, Deuteronomy 19:15-21 provides some
insight.

> A single witness is not sufficient to convict a person of any mis-
> deed or sin; this is true of any sin sinned. Only on the evidence of
> two, or even three, witnesses shall a charge stand. If a violent
> (malicious) witness comes forth to accuse someone of wrongdo-
> ing, then both parties to the dispute shall stand before YHWH,
> before the priests and the judges in office in those days, and the
> judges will make a careful inquiry. If the witness is a lying wit-
> ness, testifying with lies against the other, then you shall do to the

lying witness exactly as the lying witness meant to do to the other. Thus you shall remove the evil from your midst. The others will hear and be afraid, and an evil thing like this shall never again be done among you. You must show no pity! Life for life, eye for eye, tooth for tooth, hand for hand, foot for foot.

The very grave danger of courtroom lies is demonstrated by this passage. The cruel treatment to be meted out to the lying witness (the Exodus formulation of the ninth commandment) indicates that such an evil thing cannot be allowed to stand unpunished. It must be rooted out as the evil thing that it is.

That evil thing refers to the single witness, and suggests just why a single witness should never be enough to convict any defendant; the possibilities of error or confusion or outright lies for money or revenge make single-witness testimony finally unreliable. The passage, as a result of those dangers, says that two or even three (!) witnesses might be needed to ensure the fair adjudication of a difficult case. We know how difficult it is today to find two, much less three, reliable witnesses to a crime or wrongdoing. Think of the difficulty of proving the breaking of the seventh commandment with such a strict requirement of multiple witnesses. Adultery, after all, is the sort of thing that is rarely done in front of witnesses! And Deuteronomy's demand for multiple witnesses certainly calls into serious question the terrible scenario of testing by which a woman accused of adultery was supposedly to be tried (See Num. 5 and the discussion of the seventh commandment above). However, this text is clear in its demands; when it comes to truth no corners can be cut. Truth is central to the community, and must be achieved no matter how long it takes.

The fact that very difficult cases, not easy of adjudication, continually arose is indicated by two other Deuteronomy passages. Deuteronomy 17:8-9 commands that if any legal issue (whether concerning bloodshed or legal rights of any kind) is simply too difficult for the contesting parties or the local officials to decide, then the case must go to the priests and to the "judge who is in office in those days" (Deut. 17:9 NRSV). Apparently, the judge was an appointed official, who served a specified and limited term. His role was primarily to sit at trial over cases that could not find conclusion at the local level. And, according to Deuteronomy 1:17, Moses himself would serve as judge in the very hardest of cases.

These passages tell of the great concern Israel had for truth-telling in the court of law. One other passage is worthy of comment. The eighth century prophet Micah railed against the corruption of the Jerusalem of his day, finding the cause among three groups: the rulers, the priests, and the prophets. The first group, the rulers, the administrators of the court, the interpreters of the law, Micah claims "give judgment for a bribe" (Mic. 3:11). And there is the central problem. The demand for impartiality and truth-telling is subverted by money. Once money purchases justice, there can be no justice. The result? For Micah it can be nothing less than the end of the community. Perhaps this fact is no less true in our own time.

EXEGESIS OF THE NINTH COMMANDMENT

Five words will occupy our attention as we exegete this commandment.

1
"Answer" ('anah)

There are four meanings in Hebrew for this one root verb and considerable argument concerning how to differentiate the meanings from one another. For our concerns, the common meaning "answer" is the appropriate one. The verb, when used in general contexts of trials, as it is here, "probably derives its use (from) the context of negotiations and disputes." "The verbal response expressed by *'anah* can be evoked by an experience, a perception, or an event."[3] In the ninth commandment, the witness "answers" the question posed by the court or by his/her adversary in court. That answer must be one of absolute truth, must be neither lying nor empty. The meaning of this word is quite straightforward and needs no further example or explication.

2
"Neighbor" (rea')

The basic meaning of this common noun is: "friend, companion, fellow." This meaning is sometimes quite general, as in 2 Samuel

12:11, where Nathan curses the adulterous David by saying that his wives will be given to "his neighbor." Although this curse sounds general in chapter 12, it becomes much more specific in chapter 15 when Absalom, David's own son, only perhaps ironically his "neighbor," sleeps with David's wives after forcing him from Jerusalem. At other times the word is very much like our word "friend." Hirah is "friend" to Judah, helping him to find sexual satisfaction with a prostitute after the death of his wife. Unfortunately, his choice of sexual partner turns out to be his clever daughter-in-law, Tamar! Jonadab is "friend" to Amnon, and coaches his friend in the art of tricking and seducing his half-sister Tamar (same name, different woman!) (2 Sam. 13:3). The result of this friend's work is the ruin of Tamar and the ultimate death of Amnon at the hands of an enraged Absalom.

Of course, in other contexts the word means "fellow citizen," a person with whom one stands in some sort of reciprocal relationship. A famous example is from Job 16:21. Job hopes for a heavenly witness who would "maintain the right of a mortal with God in the same way that one does with a *neighbor*." Job is desperate to find some being who would deal with the God who now apparently hates Job, a sort of mediator who would speak on Job's behalf with the God who has taken everything from Job for no obvious reason. Likewise in Ruth 4:7, after the legal decision has been settled between Boaz and the unnamed next-of-kin, "the one took off a sandal and gave it to the other *(rea')*," that is, to one in disputed relationship with the other.

In the ninth commandment the "neighbor/friend" was clearly a person in relationship with the witness, either an actual community neighbor, living in close proximity, or at the very least a fellow citizen, a fellow member of the community. Whatever the precise relationship, the commandment calls for truth, for honest witness.

3
"Witness" ('edh)

A rather clear definition of this term is found in Leviticus 5:1. "Anyone sins if they hear a call to be a witness—and are able to see or to understand a thing—yet do not testify; they will be punished!" If one has important evidence to give, and refuses to give it though perfectly capable of doing so, that one is subject to punishment. As we have suggested already, Israel appears to intensify the demand for truthful witness in several ways. A single witness was never enough, as the careful demands on such witnesses at Deuteronomy 19:15-21 demonstrate. Then two witnesses were needed for cases where death sentences for murder were handed down (Num. 35:30). The same was true for charges of idolatry (Deut. 17:6), and to make certain that the testimony was indeed truthful in such cases, the witnesses themselves had to be the first to carry out the sentence (Deut. 17:7)! Finally, as noted above, "two or three" witnesses are said to be needed in *all* cases (Deut. 19:15).

Two prophetic texts suggest the importance of witnesses even in semi-judicial contexts. YHWH demands that Isaiah name one of his sons Maher-shalal-hash-baz ("speedy spoil, quick plunder"), to write that name on a tablet prior to the son's birth, and to get two reliable witnesses to attest to the truthfulness of the action (Isa. 8:1-3). Likewise, Jeremiah, while imprisoned during the final Babylonian siege of Jerusalem, buys a piece of family property, and signs the deed of purchase in the presence of two witnesses (Jer. 32).

Proverbs 25:18 provides clear commentary on the ninth commandment. "Like a war club, a sword, or a sharp arrow is one who bears a lying witness *('edh shaqer)* against a neighbor." The comparisons in the proverb are instructive. A "lying witness" bears the same deadly consequences as the three basic instruments of war: club, sword, and arrow. The first is brutal and often deadly; the second cuts deep and lacerates with intent to kill; the third strikes from a distance, but for all that is no less deadly. These brutal battle actions are too often matched by the mortal brutality of a lying witness.

4
"Lying" (shaqer)

The basic meaning of the word is "deception" or "falsehood." The implication is that an expected behavior does not occur; what was supposed to happen simply did not. For example, the prophet Samuel rejects Saul's attempts to explain his behavior with regard to the Amalekites by proclaiming that YHWH, "the Glory of Israel, will not lie or will not change his mind" (1 Sam. 15:29). YHWH has torn the kingdom from the failed Saul, says Samuel, and the decision is irreversible. If God did change the divine mind, Samuel equates that with a lie. Of course, some six verses later we are told that YHWH exactly *does* undergo a change of mind about Saul, a fact that could have caused the enraged Samuel no little difficulty, if he had thought about it; by his equation YHWH would then be a liar!

Also, at Proverbs 25:14 we are warned that "like clouds and wind without rain, so is someone who boasts of gift-giving without actually giving one" (lit. "a lying gift"). This proverb provides a good analogy to the expectations of the courtroom. We expect truth-telling in court; when we receive lies instead, the very universe is thrown off-kilter: windy clouds without rain, promises of gifts but no gifts, courtroom "truth" without truth. In the searing racial drama and film, *To Kill a Mockingbird*, based on the book by Harper Lee, a young woman accuses a black man of beating and raping her. Though the lawyer defending the man easily proves that his client could not have done it physically, due to the uselessness of his left arm, the all-white, all-male jury in 1932 finds the man guilty. While awaiting an appeal, the obviously innocent black man tries to escape and is killed. But in 1932 any hint of black on white sexuality and/or violence stirred emotion beyond reason. The testimony of the young woman was a pack of lies, and the truth was defeated. Thus, lying witnesses can indeed be clubs, swords, and arrows.

Hence, the Exodus version of the ninth commandment focuses on the dangers of purposeful deception when handling the truth.

5
"Empty, nothing" (sha')

We have pursued the meaning of this word in detail in connection with the discussion of the third commandment. There the commandment warned against using the sacred divine name for nothing, treating it as if it had no meaning and power. In the context of the ninth commandment, something similar is said. The testimony one provides in a courtroom is crucial and powerful. If it is treated as if it had no meaning, if its words cannot be received as truthful, then the words are in fact empty. Their impact is deception, but their content is simply empty. Such talk is less than cheap; it is worthless, not worth the breath with which it is uttered.

The difference between the words *sheqer* (in Exodus) and *sha'* (in Deuteronomy) is that the former suggests an active deception, the use of words designed directly to mislead. The young woman in *To Kill a Mockingbird* broke the Exodus version of the ninth commandment when she specifically lied about what a man had supposedly done to her when he had not done it. The latter word implies a more general worthlessness of speech. Job complains that he has been given "empty months," filled with endless nights of pain and endless days of useless struggle (Job 7:4). Such worthlessness calls into question the most basic meaning of life; if life has no meaning at all then why do we bother to live? Perhaps it could be said that the latter word is more dangerous than the former. When direct deception is uncovered, it can be questioned as an obvious evil, while the truth may then be sought with a renewed vigor. When emptiness is claimed, the very reason for anger and complaint could be said to be undermined. The author of Psalm 12 describes the dangers of empty speech very well.

> Help, O YHWH, for there are no more godly ones;
>   the faithful have disappeared from humanity!
> They speak emptiness *(sha')* to one another;
>   they communicate with double minds and
>   flattering lips. (vv. 1-2)

The result of such empty speech? "The poor are destroyed, and the needy groan." To speak emptiness leads to a basic subversion of the ways of God. The realm of God is overturned, because empty speech leads to empty ways.

It is, however, important that both versions of the ninth commandment exist in the canon. Actively deceptive speech and undermining empty speech are both rejected by this commandment, both misinformation and empty cynicism. What we say to and about one another is very important; the ninth commandment reminds us that words can be weapons of destruction and building blocks of community.

SERMONIC NOTES

1

The first sermon that presents itself on the ninth commandment could address the issues of truthful speech; why is truth-telling so central to a community? Because the great bulk of our communication with each other occurs outside the formality of a court, the question of truth in our daily dealings is crucial. This relates also to the basic notion of trust; if I cannot trust what I am being told, then how can any genuine communication occur? I have been involved with more than a few communities where lies served to undermine them, either plain falsehoods or cynical speech that create cracks and holes in the community's foundation.

Many years ago, I was a youth minister for a large congregation. Part of my responsibility was to arrange programming for Sunday evening events. There was a popular speaker, who was at that time in college, and who had come to our youth gatherings before. The youth liked him personally, and he had a warm and engaging way with them. I did not find what he had to say profound or well informed, but since he planned to attend seminary soon, he enjoyed coming as a way to get experience in speaking about his faith. I certainly did not see him as any sort of threat to my youth.

I invited him to speak one Sunday, and he readily accepted. That Sunday afternoon, he called me and said that his mother was very ill and in the hospital and that he would have to cancel his engagement with the youth. I expressed my sorrow at his mother's illness, prayed with him on the phone, and asked if I could do anything to be helpful. He said no. I hung up and quickly threw together a program for that evening.

After the program, another youth leader and I got into his car and drove eight or nine miles from the church, not thinking too carefully where we were heading. We were just talking theology, as we often did. Finally, we got hungry, and stopped for a pizza in a place we had never been. We stepped into the restaurant, and saw—the young man whose mother was supposedly very ill! There he sat with a striking woman, laughing and chatting, hardly burdened with the strain of a sick Mom. That man's lie haunts me to this day. Never again could I trust him; never again could I see him as a colleague in ministry. I have seen him several times in the ensuing years, and the scene I have described swims into my mind each time. Lies can undermine community.

2

The author of the New Testament letter of James spends an extraordinary amount of time on the tongue and its manifest dangers. "If any think they are religious, and do not bridle their tongues but deceive their hearts, their religion is worthless" (James 1:26 NRSV). "So also the tongue is a small member, yet it boasts of great exploits. How great a forest is set ablaze by a small fire! And the tongue is a fire. . . . With it (tongue) we bless the Lord and Father, and with it we curse those who are made in the likeness of God" (James 3:5-6, 9 NRSV).

Another sermon on the ninth commandment could address the dangers of empty speech, a real issue for an age overburdened with too much information and too few ways to find discernment among it. Cynical, evil speech has extraordinary power for mischief, and in a world of near-instant communication the possibilities for the spread of such speech has increased fantastically. The Internet is filled with the most incredible nonsense! Black helicopters poised to whisk millions off to prison camps prepared for the resistant in the deserts of Nevada; plots of cruel "foreigners" to poison our water supplies with incurable diseases along with directions toward safety for the few who believe aright; get-rich-quick schemes that simply cannot fail, but which can only be accessed by the few who have not been brainwashed by the government. Each of the preceding examples is actually available on the Internet, but you will have to find the addresses yourself!

Cynical and foolish speech, as much or more than deceptive speech, can undo a community's attempts to find a common ground of caring and hope for all of its members. A steady barrage of such speech from television, radio, and Internet bids to turn us into a nation of basic unbelievers, persons who trust little and fear much. The tongue is indeed a great fire, though a little member, and the origin of its cruelest speaking is nothing short of Hell itself, or so James believes (3:6). When I encounter speech like this, and one can hardly avoid it for long, it does seem as if Hell has disgorged some of its worst denizens.

3

Another sermon on the ninth commandment could address the interesting connections created by the use of the word *sha'* ("empty") both here and in the third commandment. In what ways does the empty use of YHWH's name relate to the empty use of our human speech? Is the opposite movement also true? Does empty human speech lead to empty speech about the divine? If my human communication is riddled with lies and deception, how can my speech about and to God be any different? The Ten Commandments rarely repeat words in their spare enumerations. The fact that this word is repeated when discussing the risks of empty speech about God and empty speech between human beings emphasizes the possible connections between the two forms of speaking.

I am reminded again of Amos 8. The shopkeepers, sitting in the back of the sanctuary, are anxious that the service be over so that they can go back to cheating their clients again (!). Lying speech to human beings leads to lying worship of God. Our daily speech is inexorably bound up with our speech to God; truth must characterize both. This is true both for our own spiritual health and for the spiritual health of our community.

CHAPTER TEN

The Tenth Commandment

You must not covet the house of your neighbor, nor covet the wife of your neighbor, his male or female slave, his ox, his donkey, nor anything that is your neighbor's. (Exod. 20:17)

You must not covet your neighbor's wife, and you must not desire the house of your neighbor, his field, his male or female slave, his ox or his donkey, nor anything that is your neighbor's. (Deut. 5:21)

This final commandment has proved very contentious in its explications through the centuries. The central question revolves around the meaning of the word "covet" *(chamad)*. Does the word imply an inner feeling only, or does that feeling of desire need to be matched with action to constitute a shattering of the commandment? When President Jimmy Carter was quoted in an article in *Playboy* magazine in the late 1970s, saying that "he had committed lust in his heart" (with the object of that lust unnamed!), he clearly implied that he had "coveted" another woman, but had not in any way acted on those desires. But the President obviously believed that his unannounced coveting was a breach of the seventh and the tenth commandments. For that famous Southern Baptist Christian, a stray lustful thought broke the commandments.

Such a rigorous interpretation would make sinners of us all, given as we all are to numerous lustful, violent, and other despicable thoughts nearly every day of our lives. Is that the intent of the tenth commandment? Jesus is remembered to have thought so, and his reflection on the tenth commandment was central to President

Carter's interpretation. "You have heard it said, 'You shall not commit adultery.' But I say to you that everyone who looks at a woman with lust has already committed adultery with her in his heart" (Matt. 5:27-28). Jesus here combines the seventh commandment with the tenth, suggesting that the tenth adds immeasurable danger to the more overt commands that precede it. Even *thinking* about killing, or adultery, or theft, or lying, by this way of thought, constitutes the act itself. Can it be said that this rigor is the intent of the tenth commandment? We will discuss this at greater length in the exegesis.

Another point of contention in this commandment is the two different formulations of it in Exodus and Deuteronomy. In the former, the verb "covet" controls the entire command, but in the latter the verb "covet" only is used with "neighbor's wife," while the verb "desire" (*'wh*) presides over the remainder of the neighbor's goods. Does this distinction imply that the "wife" is something different than the rest of a neighbor's "things"? This differentiation led many commentators to divide our tenth commandment into nine and ten, making "covet the wife" number nine and "desire" for the rest number ten (Luther is the classic example; John Calvin did not follow Luther in this division). This implies, perhaps, that the two Hebrew verbs are not in fact perfect synonyms. But can clear distinctions be found between them? Again, the exegesis will attempt to answer these questions.

However these exegetical questions are to be adjudicated, the idea that "wife" is lumped together with "oxen, donkeys, and slaves" has rankled more than a few women (and one hopes a few men) down through the centuries. Though Hebrew legal tradition implies again and again that women are certainly second-class beings with respect to men, this tenth commandment has been seen as a particularly memorable and unpleasant formulation of that notion. At least in the Exodus formulation of the commandment, it appears to be just as unacceptable to covet a neighbor's ox as it is to covet his wife, but no more or less unacceptable! And in Deuteronomy, desiring a field is no worse or better than coveting a wife, if the two verbs are indeed synonyms. Such language in our day would be the stuff of myriad lawsuits!

But what really is at stake in this final commandment? Is there some reason why it caps the list of ten? Exactly how is it different from the eighth commandment against stealing? A brief look at the interpretative history of the commandment may provide some clues toward answers to these questions.

THE SUBSEQUENT HISTORY OF THE TENTH COMMANDMENT

We have already referred to the Jesus tradition concerning the meaning of the tenth commandment. It is a rigorous reading indeed, and implies clearly that the word "covet" adds an inner disposition to the actual commission of an act of theft or killing or adultery. To look on a woman in lust is already to have committed adultery with her "in his heart" (Matt. 6:28). If the Greek word "heart" has its Semitic connotation of "mind/will," then private lust is equivalent to the act of lust itself. This is a high standard for human behavior, but not an unexpected one. In the same section of Matthew's gospel we are told that the "pure in heart" will see God (Matt. 5:8). The implication is that those not pure in heart will have no access to God. If one's mind is set on someone else's wife or farm or goods, then even if the thought is never turned to action, the fact of the thought blinds the thinker to the higher demands of righteousness. The one who covets quite literally loses sight of God.

This rigorous interpretation of coveting has been repeated throughout the centuries. John Calvin calls for the higher righteousness demanded by this interpretation.[1] R. H. Charles claimed that this reading of the tenth commandment "more than doubled the claims of the entire Decalogue."[2] That is to say, if my inner desire is as dangerous and potentially deadly as my actions, then even *thinking about* taking YHWH's name for nothing, or thinking about killing, is disastrous for my faith in the God who brought me out of the house of my slavery. For Charles, the commandment against coveting plays a huge role in international relations, since it is the basic desire of one nation for another nation's territory that so often leads to war. Charles published his book in 1923, just five years after the end of the massive World War that gave evidence of such greed for land and goods. Of course, Charles could not have known that while his book was being published, an unknown Austrian veteran of that great war was writing his own book, a central piece of which was his demand for *Lebensraum* (living space) for a greater Germany. No better example than Adolf Hitler could be found for the dangers of coveting and the horrors it can produce.

Edwin Poteat adds to this interpretation when he says that "coveting the wrong thing is wrong."[3] He notes that the apostle Paul, just prior to his magnificent chapter describing the "still more excellent way," warns his readers to "strive for the greater gifts" rather than for titles and power (1 Cor. 12:31). That greater gift is best exemplified by "love," more specifically the love of God revealed in Jesus Christ. That love outlasts all other gifts, enables a person to avoid the dangers of coveting, and allows one to keep eyes fixed on God. In this light, covetousness becomes "uncontrolled desire or desire off balance."[4] Nearly every commentator of the tenth commandment would agree that it warns us against improper desire focused on things to the exclusion of thoughts and actions that build and sustain the community. Poteat offers a neat paraphrase of two of the commandments to make the point. "Honor father and mother and live long; covet whatever is thy neighbor's and die soon."[5] The sharp contrast between the two verbs "honor" and "covet" tells the reader that both thoughts and actions can be turned either to evil or good for the community; the latter kills while the former makes alive.

Some have suggested that the tenth commandment is distinctly different from the previous nine, because it adds intention to the list of actions that are proscribed. To the contrary, I would argue that this commandment is reminiscent of the first commandment's demand that only YHWH be worshiped. All other would-be gods are rejected, and not simply the active practice of their worship. If one takes with final seriousness the call of the God who brought us out of Egypt, both interiorly and exteriorly one is bound to follow this God alone. A believer who has been grasped by that God must have her thoughts and her actions fixed on the ways and demands of that God to the exclusion of all other thoughts and actions. It could rightly be said that the tenth commandment only states explicitly what the first said implicitly: both thoughts and actions must be directed by and to YHWH, the savior and redeemer.

EXEGESIS OF THE TENTH COMMANDMENT

1
"Covet" (chamad)

The meaning of this word "covers the entire human sequence from viewing through perception of pleasure or even delight and

inward longing to the desire to possess and the act of possession."
There remains some dispute concerning whether in every case the
action of taking possession is included, but it cannot be doubted
that "the desire for an object or person expressed by *chamad* has
such possession as its goal."[6] When understood in this comprehen-
sive way, the use of the verb appears to be a window onto typical
human behavior, whether in the ancient world or in our own; no
clear distinction can or should be made between the obsessive
desire for a thing and the obtaining of the thing itself. Two texts
make the point.

We have discussed the story of Achan in connection with the
commandment against stealing, but one sentence of that story
nicely summarizes the sequence of covetous thinking that lead him
to the act of theft. "I saw among the spoil a lovely cloak from
Shinar, along with two hundred shekels of silver, and a bar of gold
weighing fifty shekels. So, I coveted *(chamad)* them and took them"
(Josh. 7:21). Even as Achan recounts his crime, a crime that will
lead to his death and the death of his family, he lingers over the
objects taken, telling Joshua that he had been seduced by their
beauty, a beauty he relishes even now. The cloak of Shinar was
"lovely," and the silver and gold were carefully weighed; Achan
remembers with genuine pleasure the exact weight of the desired
silver and gold coins and bars. The dazzling goods lead him precisely to "covet" them and finally to "take" them.

The second text is the famous story of the garden in Eden. There
too the movement of seeing, coveting, and taking can be witnessed.
"When the woman saw that the tree was good for eating, and that
it was a delight (from the root *'wh*) to the eyes, and that the tree was
coveted to make a person wise, she took of its fruit and ate, and
gave some to her man with her, and he ate" (Gen. 3:6). Note here
how the simple act of observation of the tree, that unique tree
planted by YHWH in the middle of the garden, turns to "coveting"
after the snake's revelation of the special nature of the tree. And, in
turn, the coveting, "which takes possession of someone and incor-
porates the deed within itself,"[7] leads to taking, "despite the best
will and intentions." Wallis suggests quite helpfully that English
has a phrase which captures something of the meaning of covet in
the tenth commandment: "have one's eye on something."[8] When
we say, "I've had my eye on that for some time," we generally
mean that we have just purchased it (or, heaven forbid, stolen it!)

or intend to do so very soon. Here again the sight leads to the desire leads to the possession.

2
"desire" ('wh)

Mayer in TDOT states flatly that "'wh is synonymous with *chamad*."[9] He notes the parallelism of the two words in Genesis 3:6 (see above), and points to a comparison of Psalm 68:17 (Eng. v. 16) and Psalm 132:13. In the former psalm it states, "the mountain that God coveted *(chamad)* for a dwelling," with reference to the hill of Zion. In Psalm 132, it says, "Because YHWH chose Zion, desired *('wh)* it for a dwelling." I would suggest that neither example is especially compelling. In the former, we saw above that the "seeing" led to "desire" and then to "coveting." Because that sequence is clear, there is no reason why the two verbs should be seen as synonymous at all. And in the latter example, the contexts of the two psalms are quite distinct: two different names for God are used as well as two different names for "dwelling." This is hardly proof of synonymity. If there is no certain proof that the words mean the same thing, then the addition in Deuteronomy may have a different rationale. In the lengthy story of the people's demands for meat in Numbers 11:4-35, they distrust the leadership of God and attempt to do "what they desire." After the people's continuous demand for meat, in place of the tiresome manna, YHWH sends quail, two cubits deep, which they gather for thirty-six hours and begin to consume. But in the midst of the barbecue, while the meat was still being chewed, YHWH struck the faithless ones with plague; many died. The name of this awful place became "The Graves of Desire," because there the people who had the "desire" were buried (Num. 11:34). The meaning of the word "desire" in this story appears to be synonymous with human self-assertiveness, a rebellion against God. Might not that meaning be important for the formulation of the commandment in Deuteronomy?

Since the book of Deuteronomy is framed as a series of sermons by Moses to the people of Israel, the addition of the word "desire" with the sense of rebellion against God would add to the sermonic quality of the commandment. Not only are we warned that "coveting" is dangerous for the community, but also if we "desire" things of our neighbors we rebel against our God. The "desire" of the woman in Genesis 3:6 may be another example of this notion of rebellion against the command of God. By the use of these two words, the commandment regulates both the community and our relationship to the God who forms the community. Thus, the two words are not strictly synonyms in the Deuteronomy version of the tenth commandment; they are complementary terms, reinforcing one another in the attempt to form proper community under God and to shape proper behavior in relationship to God.

Another observation concerning the differences between the two formulations is that Deuteronomy adds to the list of things not be desired the "field" of the neighbor. Again, this is a special concern of Deuteronomy. Many of the laws enshrined in the book have to do with land tenure and use, both crucial concerns to an agricultural community. For example, at 11:15, Israel is promised that if they follow the commandments of God, God will give them rain "for the grass of your fields for your livestock."

One can also find an important commentary on the tenth commandment in the eighth-century Micah. At Micah 2:1-2, the prophet announces disaster for certain members of the comfortable class in Jerusalem.

> Woe to you planners of evil,
> doers of evil while still in bed!
> When the light appears, they do it,
> because they are their own gods!
> They covet fields, then grab them,
> and houses, then take them away.
> They oppress landowner and household,
> everyone and their inheritance!

Once again, we see the movement of activity in connection with the word "covet." First, these evil people "plan while still in bed," then they "covet," and finally they grab both houses and fields, two objects from the Deuteronomy list of the tenth commandment. And Micah says that the basic reason for this appalling behavior is that "they are their own gods." The literal Hebrew is: "they have in their hands a god." The NRSV's reading, "because it is in their power," conceals the clearer connection to the Ten Commandments that Micah intends. These evil thieves have rejected the first commandment, taking themselves as gods, or perhaps choosing other gods. The result of their rejection of YHWH is the shattering of the eighth and the tenth commandments. Micah illustrates very well the absolute necessity of embracing the first commandment before one can hope to follow the other nine. His is an early sermon, demonstrating the important connections among the entire list of ten.

SERMONIC NOTES

1

A sermon based on the tenth commandment could revolve around the fascinating insights surrounding the rich meanings of the central word, "covet." Since the word in the Hebrew Bible includes all the inner movements of thought and feeling that precede evil actions, a preacher could hold up his own behaviors, and those of his congregation, in the mirror of, for example, the story of Achan's theft. Just as Achan "saw" and "desired" and "took," so we "see" the ubiquitous advertising of our day, are aroused by it to fuel our desires, and are pushed toward "taking" things we hardly need. The Scripture's insights into the question of coveting are deeper than the simple notion that we tend to want too much stuff. It helps us to see more clearly just why we do want too much, and to see how the excesses of our greed actually happen.

Of course, both in the cases of Achan and Micah's prophetic outburst, those railed against are overt thieves. Few of us are such overt thieves. At least no court of law would brand us so. Yet, the preacher may need to expand the congregation's definition of theft to include more of them than they originally thought. I write these words (May, 2001) while the current United States government is wrestling with an energy policy for the country. That government is concerned to open up more places for oil and gas exploration and to expand the use of coal-fired and nuclear-powered generating plants. This emphasis, at least currently, has led to de-emphasizing conservation measures to save precious power. One administration official, while in effect rejecting increased emphasis on conservation, said that "our American heritage" would be threatened if absolutely free choice in the purchase of vehicles, or the setting of thermostats, were in any way threatened. The increasing production and purchase of huge Sport Utility Vehicles, many of which get ten miles to the gallon or fewer, was to him merely part of the American way of life. Lost in all that rhetoric is the simple fact that we citizens of the United States, representing about 6 percent of the world's population (and shrinking), use upwards of 25 percent of the world's energy. Does this constitute a breaking of the eighth commandment as well as the tenth? Is Micah close to the truth when he accuses the comfortable of his day with "choosing their own gods," and by implication rejecting YHWH?

2

The dangers of "coveting" are both individual *and* corporate. Sermons in twenty-first century pulpits must never tire of announcing this important truth. The modern church has too often made the assumption that the Bible was written for the individual believer, and that if I get right with God then my community will be a better place. This is no doubt true, as far as it goes. But it must be remembered and announced that there are in fact few if any individual truths in the Scriptures. All biblical truth is finally cor- porate. Hence, when we invoke the tenth commandment (or any of the other nine), we are inevitably talking about the shape of a whole community as much as we are talking about the shape of any individual. The above example about our profligate use of energy is a classic case of a corporate shattering of the tenth com- mandment. How could any reasonable Christian or Jew or Muslim believer defend such absurd disparities between our United States population and its disproportionate use of the world's energy? Thus, it is not merely my individual greed and lusty desire for things (though I am surely individually greedy and lusty!) that is at stake in the tenth commandment; I live in a country of greed and lust. How can my church, my neighborhood, and my country bring themselves more in line with the will of God for equality and wholeness in the world God has created and redeemed? A sermon with this concern might want to focus on issues of ecology.

3

A sermon on the dangers of "just" coveting could be important. Jesus' claims about "lusting in the heart" being equivalent to the action of lusting itself is worth some thought. It is far more than a "conservative" reading of the seventh and tenth commandments. His reading seems to imply that continuous coveting of someone else or someone else's things crowds out thoughts that can serve to uplift the spirit and the life of the community. The beatitude that states, "Happy are the pure in heart, for they shall see God," suggests that purity of heart (i.e., single-mindedness) leads one to a vision of God. It also suggests that a mind clouded with covetous desires is blinded to God's presence.

Such a sermon could ask: with what are we filling our minds? Preachers need to be careful here not to descend to moralisms like: "avoid the lewd and search for the wholesome," or "let's burn the smutty books and records and watch only reruns of *Touched by an Angel*." However, questions concerning viewing and reading habits can and should be raised. I am personally much more concerned about violence in the media than I am about pornography, although both are very dangerous. In a country where nearly thirteen thousand people were killed in 1999 by gunfire, and where millions of guns are in the hands of citizens, what are we learning, and teaching our children, about violence as a way to solve problems? Is there too much violence in our movies, or on our TVs? Are guns seen more and more to be the "equalizer" in a dangerous world? How many crimes are prevented by the ownership of a gun over against crimes committed by means of a gun? How can we focus our minds on the things of God when we are sated with the things of the world: violence, sex, and toys, both child and adult? In short, attention to the importance of the first commandment can lead us to a right understanding of the "pure in heart," which in turn can lead to a vision of God and a clearer understanding of God's vision for us.

Some Final Reflections

"It is a monstrous distortion of who and what [God] is to think that the self-revelation which took place on Sinai was nothing more than the proclamation of a legalistic code."[1] Christian preachers have the continual task of retraining their congregations about the basic substance of the Jewish tradition, the root from which the Christian branch has grown. Sermons on the Ten Commandments can help to perform this task.

In the material I have shared in the preceding chapters, I have tried regularly to tease out possible contemporary applications of the ancient words. And I have simultaneously tried to connect the Ten with one another, so that you can see that they are far more than individual laws designed to stop our terrible human behaviors. As much as we need all the help we can get to curb our all-too-common greed and lust and exploitations of one another, we need a clear sense of just how we can avoid all that. The Ten Commandments urge us to a commitment to the loving and challenging God who brought us out of the land of Egypt. Once that commitment is announced and affirmed, we can turn to the specific demands that commitment entails. "A commandment such as 'You must not commit adultery' is not an enslavement but a liberation, not a threat to freedom but a means to freedom, not a thwarting of life's flowering but an incentive to the flowering of human relations, including sexual relations."[2] In short, the Ten Commandments are God's good gift to the community that is called by God's name to become a "kingdom of priests and a holy nation."

We Christians would do well to remember that the most joyous celebration in Judaism is the yearly feast of *Simchat Torah*, "the joy of Torah." On this wild festival day, the Torah scroll is removed from the synagogue and in a long and exuberant parade through the streets of the city, is passed from hand to hand through the crowd. All the while, there is much singing and drinking and dancing. I was privileged some years ago to be in Tiberius, Israel on *Simchat Torah*. I will never forget the wild joy of the people as they danced through their streets to their holy cemetery, which contains the bodies of some of Judaism's most revered figures, the great twelfth-century thinker Maimonides among them. After witnessing that energetic parade, and all the joyful faces streaked with sweat, I could never again think that the Torah was a burden for Jews. The Torah was gift, that much was obvious to me that day. Similarly, the Ten Commandments are God's gift, not only to the Jews, but to us who would claim that we have been rescued from our slavery, brought out of bondage by a mighty hand, and have been promised a new land. In that new land we are commanded by that God to live together in a community of justice and righteousness. The Ten are the foundation document for that new community.

I once listened (in some pain!) to a student sermon that attempted to address all ten commandments. I remember chiding the student for attempting to do too much in one sermon, which is a common enough criticism in my teaching. I urged him to take them one at a time, giving each one a fuller reflection, focusing the congregation's attention on the one theme of the one command-ment for that day. I still think that is good advice. Every preacher needs to have a series on the Ten Commandments at least every several years; interest and curiosity in them never seems to flag, and much mischief continues to be done in their name.

However, I would now add that before the series begins, the preacher needs to introduce them as a whole list. Under a title like "The Ten Commandments for Today," the preacher should help the congregation see that the Ten have a purposeful shape, beginning with the all-important first that urges single-minded commitment to the God who has claimed us, and ending with the certainty that the claim of God covers all of our thoughts and actions, both interior and exterior. These Ten Commandments are hardly all we need to know about the rule of God in our lives, but they are a wonderful starting point for us to discover, or to rediscover, just what it is God wants from us, as well as just what it is that God has done for us. "Israel certainly did not understand the Decalogue as an absolute moral law prescribing ethics: she rather recognised it as a revelation vouch-safed to her at a particular moment in her history, through which she was offered the saving gift of life."[3] But not just Israel. We Christians, who appropriate the words of the Hebrew Bible as a word for us, can also hear in these Ten the saving gift of life for us, made complete in the life, death, and resurrection of Jesus.

Our age needs the Ten Commandments again, but not as sterile laws, hung on school room doors and court room walls. We need the living and vital Ten Commandments, all Ten, to remind us of the God who gave them and to remind us of what that God wants us finally to become.

Notes

Preface

1. Martin Luther, *The Large Catechism*, translated by Robert H. Fische (Philadelphia: Muhlenberg, 1959), 5.

2. R. H. Charles, *The Decalogue* (Edinburgh: T&T Clark, 1923), 185.

3. Walter Harrelson, *The Ten Commandments and Human Rights* (Philadelphia: Fortress, 1980), 47.

1. The First Commandment

1. I have chosen to indicate the *divine tetragrammaton,* the mysterious four-consonant name for God, in this unpronounceable way, both to duplicate its look on the page of the Hebrew text and to honor those Jews who, for religious reasons, refuse to utter the name aloud. The NRSV translation renders it LORD.

2. Andrew Greeley, *The Sinai Myth* (Garden City, N.Y.: Doubleday, 1972), 54.

3. Ibid., 23-24.

4. See, among many others, the discussion of the origins of the Ten Commandments in Harrelson, *The Ten Commandments*, 19-48.

2. The Second Commandment

1. R. H. Charles, *The Decalogue*, 76-88.

2. Stanley M. Hauerwas and William H. Willimon, *The Truth About God* (Nashville: Abingdon, 1999), 25-26.

3. Chaim Potok, *My Name is Asher Lev* (New York: Fawcett Crest, 1970).

4. G. Johannes Botterweck and Helmer Ringgren, editors, *Theological Dictionary of the Old Testament* (TDOT), (Grand Rapids: Eerdmans), vol. V, 1986, Hans-Jürgen Zobel, 62.

5. Luther, *The Large Catechism*, 9.

6. Greeley, *Sinai Myth*, 110.

7. Brevard S. Childs, *The Book of Exodus* (Philadelphia: Westminster, 1974), 66.

8. Ibid., 67.

3. The Third Commandment

1. Andrew Greeley, *Sinai Myth*, 123.
2. William Barclay, *The Ten Commandments for Today* (New York: Harper & Row, 1973), 25.
3. Charles, *The Decalogue*, 89.
4. Edwin McNeill Poteat, *Mandate to Humanity* (Nashville: Abingdon, 1953), 116.
5. Luther, *Large Catechism*, 15.
6. Childs, *Exodus*, 68.
7. G. Warmuth, *TDOT*, vol. IX, 556.

4. The Fourth Commandment

1. Charles, *The Decalogue*, 115.
2. Poteat, *Mandate*, 127.
3. Luther, *Large Catechism*, 22.
4. Barclay, *The Ten*, 37.
5. H. Eising, *TDOT*, vol. IV, 67.

5. The Fifth Commandment

1. Luther, *Large Catechism*, 23.
2. Ibid., 28.
3. John Calvin, *The Institutes of the Christian Religion*, translated by Ford Lewis Battles (Philadelphia: Westminster, 1960), 375.
4. Ibid., 402.
5. Poteat, *Mandate*, 140.
6. Harrelson, *The Ten Commandments*, 93.
7. Ibid., 95.
8. Childs, *Exodus*, 72.
9. Josef Pløger, *TDOT*, vol. I, 96.
10. Harrelson, *The Ten Commandments*, 103.
11. Ibid., 104.
12. Ibid., 104.

6. The Sixth Commandment

1. Hauerwas and Willimon, *The Truth*, 80.
2. Harrelson, *The Ten Commandments*, 113.
3. Hauerwas and Willimon, *The Truth*, 80.
4. Luther, *Large Catechism*, 33.
5. Ibid., 35.
6. Ibid., 35.
7. Charles, *The Decalogue*, 192.
8. Poteat, *Mandate*, 162-65.
9. Clovis Chappell, *Ten Rules for Living* (Nashville: Cokesbury, 1938), 87.
10. Hauerwas and Willimon, *The Truth*, 84.

7. The Seventh Commandment

1. Harrelson, *The Ten Commandments*, 124.
2. Luther, *Large Catechism*, 36
3. Poteat, *Mandate*, 177.
4. Ibid., 168.
5. Chappell, *Ten Rules*, 104.
6. Charles, *The Decalogue*, 213.
7. D. N. Freedman and B. E. Willoughby, *TDOT*, vol. IX, 114.
8. Renita J. Weems, *Battered Love* (Minneapolis: Fortress, 1995).
9. See Dan Jacobson, *The Rape of Tamar* (New York: Macmillan, 1970) for a powerful fictional retelling of this gruesome story.

8. The Eighth Commandment

1. See V. Hamp, *TDOT*, vol. III, 40 for further details.
2. Ibid., 40.
3. Walter Eichrodt, "The Law and the Prophets," *Interpretation*, vol. II, 1957, 38.
4. Luther, *Large Catechism*, 39.
5. Harrelson, *The Ten Commandments*, 137.
6. Charles, *The Decalogue*, 229.
7. Chappell, *Ten Rules*, 116.
8. Poteat, *Mandate*, 189.
9. Ibid., 191.
10. V. Hamp, *TDOT*, vol. III, 41.
11. Ibid., 44.

9. The Ninth Commandment

1. Luther, *Large Catechism*, 43.
2. Chappell, *Ten Rules*, 132.
3. F. J. Stendebach, *TDOT*, vol. XI, 219.

10. The Tenth Commandment

1. John Calvin, *John Calvin's Sermons on the Ten Commandments*, translated by Benjamin Farley (Grand Rapids: Baker Book House, 1980), 232-33.
2. Charles, *The Decalogue*, 260.
3. Poteat, *Mandate*, 205.
4. Ibid., 211.
5. Ibid., 215.
6. G. Wallis, *TDOT*, vol. IV, 454.
7. Ibid., 457.
8. Ibid., 455.
9. Günter Mayer, *TDOT*, vol. I, 135.

Some Final Reflections

1. Greeley, *Sinai Myth*, 215.
2. Harrelson, *The Ten Commandments*, 187.
3. Gerhard von Rad, *Old Testament Theology*, translated by D. M. G. Stalker (New York: Harper & Row, 1962), 193-94.